QUILT MODERN CURVES
& BOLD STRIPES

15 Dynamic Projects for All Skill Levels

HEATHER BLACK AND DAISY ASCHEHOUG

stashBOOKS.
an imprint of C&T Publishing

Text copyright © 2020 by Heather Black and Daisy Aschehoug

Photography and artwork copyright © 2020 by C&T Publishing, Inc.

Publisher: Amy Barrett-Daffin

Creative Director: Gailen Runge

Acquisitions Editor: Roxane Cerda

Managing Editor: Liz Aneloski

Editor: Karla Menaugh

Technical Editors: Del Walker and Debbie Rodgers

Cover/Book Designer: April Mostek

Production Coordinator: Zinnia Heinzmann

Production Editor: Alice Mace Nakanishi

Illustrator: Aliza Shalit

Photo Assistant: Rachel Holmes

Lifestyle photography by Kelly Burgoyne and Christina Carty-Francis; subjects photography by Diane Pedersen, Kelly Burgoyne, and Rachel Holmes; and instructional photography by Rachel Holmes and Kelly Burgoyne of C&T Publishing, Inc., unless otherwise noted

Published by Stash Books, an imprint of C&T Publishing, Inc., P.O. Box 1456, Lafayette, CA 94549

Library of Congress Control Number:2019946321

Printed in China

10 9 8 7 6 5 4 3 2 1

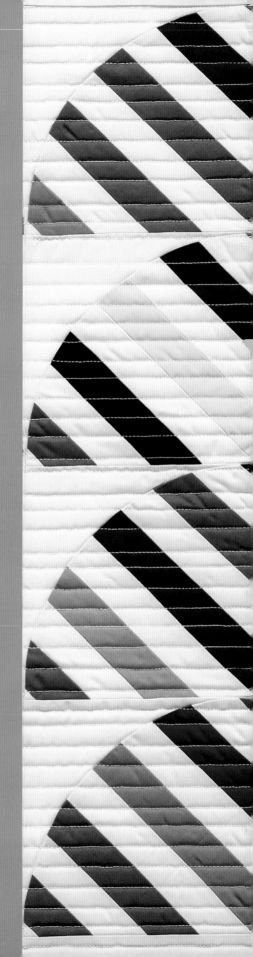

DEDICATIONS

I would like to dedicate this book to my daughter, CoraJoan, who showed more patience than believable for a five-year-old; my parents, Cory and Joan, who have always encouraged my creativity; and my late husband, Stephen, who knew me best. I would like to praise God for making me who I am and who I will be: "being confident of this very thing, that He who has begun a good work in you will complete it until the day of Jesus Christ." Phil. 1:6 (*NKJV*)

—*Heather Black*

For my parents,
Charles and Antoinette.

—*Daisy Aschehoug*

ACKNOWLEDGMENTS

Several companies provided products that made our projects so much easier. Many thanks to Aurifil, OLFA, Sewline, Soak, and The Warm Company. All the fabrics used in our quilts are from Robert Kaufman Fabrics, and we appreciated Yael Kaufman's attentiveness as we worked through what we needed for all these quilts.

Also …

I would like to acknowledge The Modern Quilt Guild, Vivika Hansen DeNegre, and Kristine Lundblad in their encouragement of my pattern writing, my coauthor for reaching out to me and partnering on this adventure together, and how amazing and encouraging I've found the modern quilting community.   —*Heather Black*

I'd like to acknowledge Heather Black for being the best teammate and coauthor ever—I'm so inspired by you. To Rachel Justus, who stood by me in front of her longarm in the wee hours of so many nights; I can't thank you enough for being my mentor. To all the magazine editors who were willing to take my designs and support my creative journey. To Anne Bergen who ushered me into the Oslo quilting community and made sure I felt at home. And to my husband—there just aren't enough words to thank you for everything you do.   —*Daisy Aschehoug*

CONTENTS

Foreword   6

Introduction   7

GETTING STARTED   8

Choosing Fabrics
and Projects   8

Tools   11

Cutting Techniques   13
Templates

Piecing Basics   15
Curves • Quarter-circles
Double quarter-circles

Sewing Stripes   21

PROJECTS   22

Patterns   122

About the Authors   128

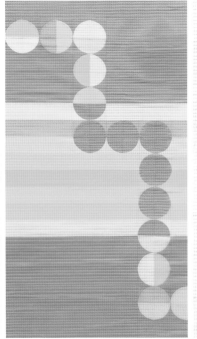

Retro Spin   22

Lys   30

Perfect Dozen   36

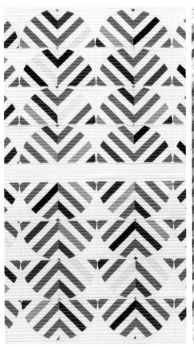

Portals   66

Prevailing Winds   74

Concert   80

Rouched   86

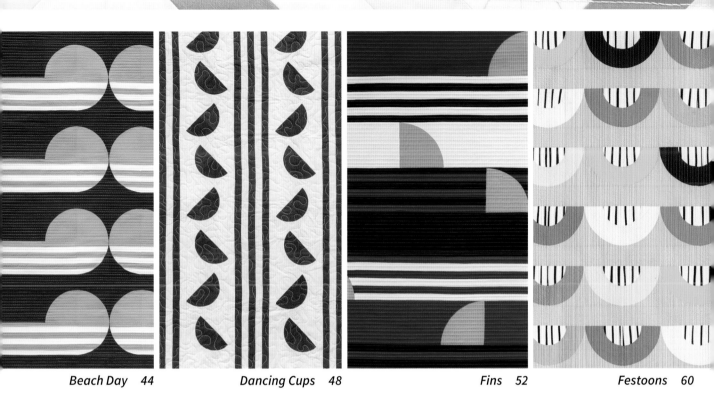

Beach Day   44   *Dancing Cups*   48   *Fins*   52   *Festoons*   60

Sunset Horizons   92   *Tidbits*   100   *Aurora*   106   *Patio Lights*   114

 # FOREWORD

Like most modern quilters, I came to the craft by way of traditional quilt-making. I loved—and still love—the time-tested patterns, elegant blocks, and rich history of quilting. I read every book I could find on the subject and experimented with multiple techniques. I was hooked, and covered each bed in my home with a traditional quilt. But eventually, I wanted more.

Luckily for me and for all of us who love modern design, the Modern Quilt Movement was born. Fresh fabrics, bold and graphic designs, and the fearless breaking of the rules (press those seams open!) of this movement breathed new life into quilting. And you're about to meet two designers who have not only embraced this aesthetic, but also influenced its widespread appeal with their innovative and award-winning quilts.

Daisy and Heather may work on different continents, but they share an instinctive understanding of the value of great design. Their work is unique, distinctive, and elegant. Both of them are masters of precision, creating quilts that pack a graphic punch as well as a sense of subtlety. And when it comes to creating curves and inserting stripes, they know when to piece, and when to step back and let the fabric do the design work for them.

It has been a privilege and an honor to work with these two creative quilters and follow the trajectory of their careers over the past five years. I can't wait to see where their talent takes them!

Best,

Vivika Hansen DeNegre
Editor, *Quilting Arts Magazine*

INTRODUCTION

As quilt designers, we found each other on Instagram through our love of curved piecing in quilts. We followed each other on social media, and when Daisy almost moved to the state of Washington where Heather lives, our friendship grew stronger over discussions about life in the northwest. Daisy ended up moving to Norway instead, but when the topic of a shared book came up, we decided the distance would simply add to an already complementary design aesthetic. We have distinct styles and perspectives, but we always come back to a shared love of curves.

For this book, we both developed designs that pair exact circles, half-circles, and quarter-circles with bold lines and stripes. Sometimes the lines stretch across circles. Sometimes the lines are contained within circles. Sometimes the two never intersect, but the straight and the curved lines always complement each other. We've treated the quilt like a canvas, and we're excited to see the masterpieces you create.

This book has block-based patterns, patterns with improvisational piecing, patterns with complex piecing, and patterns simple enough for beginners. It's a mix of everything we love about curves and stripes, and we hope there's something everyone can enjoy.

CHOOSING FABRICS AND PROJECTS

Selecting Fabrics

No matter the design, the right fabric and color choices are essential to a successful quilt. Who decides what's "right?"

You do!

If you find a pleasing palette or include much-loved fabrics, then your quilt will surely be a winner. However, there are a few tips that may help you select a combination of fabrics that are sure to be pleasant when you step back and look at your finished efforts.

Deciding on Your Palette

While planning the quilt palette, stage strips of your fabrics to see how they'll look next to each other. Many patterns call for alternating colors, and it can be helpful to see how a strip set will look by arranging strips beforehand.

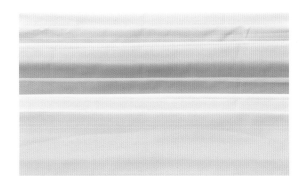

Consider prints carefully. With the exception of ombrés, solids automatically offer a consistent color. Some prints read as a single color too, and this can be helpful for adding interest without creating chaos in the final look of the quilt.

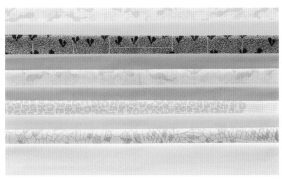

A print with one color and a neutral can read as a single color from a distance. Other prints that make sparing use of multiple colors may also create this effect.

Don't let this dissuade you from using some large-scale prints! A wild print with a lot of colors and shapes and lines can be exciting when paired with a solid. The solid gives the print a little room to breathe and allows it to get the full attention it needs. Be careful with large-scale prints that change colors over the course of a large repeat; the final look of your quilt might seem unbalanced if you haven't anticipated how the different colors will be placed throughout your quilt.

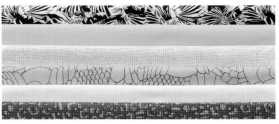

Large-scale prints paired with a solid can work well in the right pattern. Try *Dancing Cups* (page 48) or slip a few large-scale prints into the strips in *Aurora* (page 106).

Sewing with Various Fabric Types

Quilting cottons hold their shape well while also draping nicely in a finished quilt. You can easily substitute a striped fabric for pieced stripes, as long as it's printed on quilting cotton.

Lighter fabrics such as lawns, voiles, or shirting material need to be pressed with starch or a nonstarch alternative, such as Flatter (by Soak), to help them hold their shape. The thinner material can often shift when cutting and sewing. To prevent warping of lines in strip sets, add body or stiffness with a starch before you cut. Without the stiffener, the strips may appear wavy or the strips could finish in different sizes than intended.

Knits are not recommended.

Selecting a Project

Some quilts like *Beach Day* (page 44), *Fins* (page 52), and *Festoons* (page 60) make use of high-contrast strip sets. Bold colors are paired with white solids, and the result is a strong, crisp line.

The lines inside the curves of *Festoons* are black and white—maximum contrast!

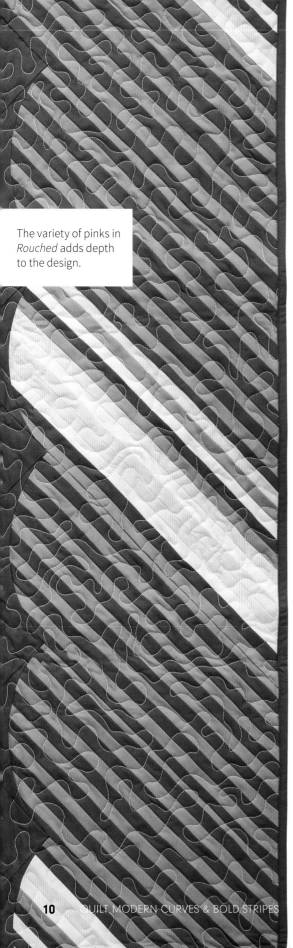

The variety of pinks in *Rouched* adds depth to the design.

Several quilts use subtler tonal shifts in the stripes. *Lys* (page 30), *Rouched* (page 86), and *Patio Lights* (page 114) are monochromatic, and the small shifts in color and value create a subtle almost texture-like effect.

Somewhere between tonal and contrasting stripes are really interesting multi or two-color variations. *Retro Spin* (page 22), *Portals* (page 66), and *Tidbits* (page 100) find balance by using two colors. Heather samples from an almost rainbow for the bold lines in *Aurora* (page 106).

Use Heather's almost-rainbow choices or pick your own palette to contrast against the curves in *Aurora*.

TOOLS

Having the right tools makes a project all the more enjoyable.
Here are some of the options we recommend.

Marking Tools

Quilters mark fabric for a variety of reasons. Some quilters outline their templates onto fabric with a marking tool before cutting. When sewing curves, some techniques require matching the center of both pieces, and marking that center first is helpful.

Local quilt shops and large craft chains have loads of marking utensils. There are pencils, pens, wash-away markers, iron-away markers, chalk sticks and chalk wheels, plastic markers for making creases, and so on. Even a bar of soap can be used to mark fabric; the soap leaves a waxy mark that washes away in the first wash. Some marking utensils will work on both light and dark fabric. Some dark marking tools will be visible only on light fabric. Trial and error will help you find the product that works for you.

Heather finger-presses her curved pieces to mark the center. Daisy uses a variety of tools, depending on what isn't lost under scrap piles in her studio— a Hera Marker, a pink or white chalk pencil, a piece of chalk, and sometimes a regular pencil.

Cutting Tools

Each quilt pattern in this book requires cutting fabric strips and template-size curved pieces. Rotary cutters are the most popular choice for these tasks. Large-diameter cutters (60 mm) are best for longer strips. Smaller cutters (28 mm) are best for curves. The standard rotary cutter size is 45 mm and is good for both strips and large, gentle curves. When cutting steep curves like the ones you find in small circles, the 28 mm is almost essential for achieving accuracy. Heather and Daisy both regularly use two sizes of rotary cutters: 28 mm and 45 mm.

Some quilters prefer to trace templates onto fabric and then cut the fabric with scissors. This will take much longer than using a rotary cutter, but it is a perfectly acceptable way to cut the pieces.

Templates

The simplest way to make a template from a pattern is to photocopy or trace it from the pages of the book onto paper. Another option includes tracing onto template plastic, which is a little thicker than paper. Once the template is cut from the plastic, it tends to last longer, but the plastic can still be cut by accident with a rotary cutter.

The most durable and reliable material for template use is acrylic. Several quilters offer their own acrylic templates including Jenny Haynes (pappersaxsten.com), Jen Carlton Bailey (bettycrockerass.com), and Sharon McConnell (colorgirlquilts.com).

Basting Tools

Three techniques for sewing curves include sewing two pieces without basting, basting with pins, and gluing fabric together. When getting started, basting with pins can seem slow. But with practice, Heather swears you can get pretty fast. Daisy always uses glue sticks / pens for basting curves. Securing fabric with a wash-away glue pen means there's less fussing with the fabric as it moves under the presser foot.

Pressing Tools

The techniques in this book demand a fair bit of precision. Using a starch or nonstarch alternative reduces slipping when pinning and sewing.

Pick and choose the tools that work best for your sewing style.

CUTTING TECHNIQUES

All the patterns for the concave, convex, and arc shapes are in the back of this book (page 122). You can choose from several different methods to make templates from the patterns and cut out your fabric.

Make Your Own Templates

1. Trace and cut the pattern from your preferred template medium (paper or thin plastic)

2. Following the placement diagrams in each project, use the paper or thin plastic template to trace the pattern onto the fabric. Cut the fabric shape with scissors or a rotary cutter, using the traced pattern as a guide.

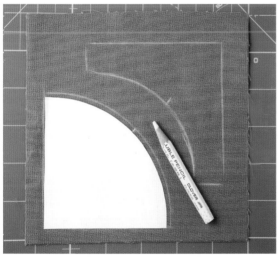

Be sure to transfer notch from the pattern onto your preferred template medium.

TIP

With practice, you can use a straight ruler to guide the rotary cutter by sliding the ruler as you cut the curve. Remember, at any given point, a curve is exactly like a straight line (until you get to the next point).

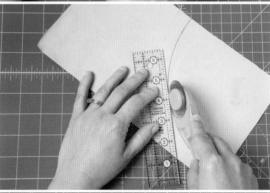

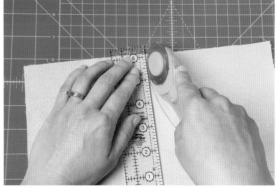

Commercial Acrylic Templates

If you decide to buy acrylic templates, take care to match the template size to the pattern in the book. Our patterns are named for their finished size and include ¼″ seam allowances around shapes. So, for example, our 6″ Concave pattern (page 124) is 6½″ from edge to edge. Some commercial acrylic templates will also produce a 6″ finished block exactly like our patterns, but they may be called 6½″ templates instead of 6″, or some other name. If you decide to buy an acrylic template, look for the finished size of the template not including seam allowances, to compare it to our patterns.

And note that some commercial templates build in *more* than a ¼″ seam allowance. When using these, adjust your fabric purchases to allow for cutting bigger shapes.

1. Refer to the template cutting guides (below) or the cutting guide in the project instructions for the most efficient use of fabric as you cut the concave and convex shapes.

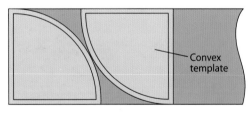

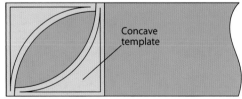

Template cutting guides. For the most efficient use of your fabric, use these cutting layouts unless otherwise directed in the pattern.

TIP
Sometimes, strip sets will be directional. Take note and orient your template accordingly.

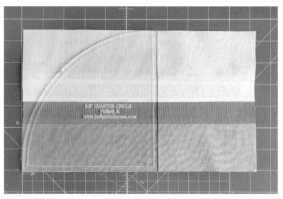

Place the template on the strip set so that the long, horizontal side of the template matches the correct color on the strip set.

2. Mark the center, using the notch in the pattern. Place your mark less than ¼″ from the edge of the fabric so it will be hidden in the seam allowance. Even if you're using a wash-away marker or chalk, there's no downside to being extra careful. Another option is to finger-press a crease at the center of the curve instead of using a marking tool.

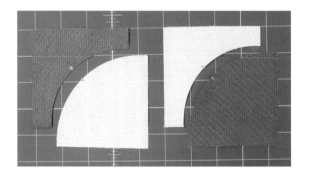

PIECING BASICS

Piecing Curves

Curves can be intimidating, and for many people it's the fear of the unknown that keeps them from ever attempting curve piecing. Curve piecing or sewing on a curve is basically the same as straight stitching—you take it one stitch at a time. You may start slow, but with practice, sewing a curve will soon be almost as quick as sewing a straight seam.

Curve Mechanics

There are two parts to any curved unit—the concave curve and the convex curve. If you are having trouble remembering the difference, here's something a teacher of Heather's once said to illustrate the difference: The concave curve makes the opening of a cave and, well, the convex doesn't.

The concave and convex curves always differ in size after adding the seam allowances. When you add the seam allowances, the concave is ½″ smaller than the convex curve. Again, to use the illustration of a cave—if you wanted to entirely block the mouth of a cave would you use a stone smaller or larger than the opening? Larger, of course. This is important to remember when creating your own quarter-circle templates.

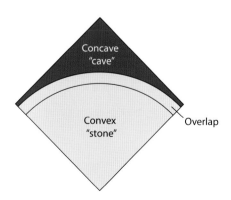

Successful Curve Piecing

A few tricks will aid in successfully sewing curves.

- If your sewing machine has a speed function, turning down the maximum sewing speed will keep you from losing control while manipulating the fabric under the presser foot. If your machine does not have this function, you can increase your control by shortening your stitch length. Doing both, slowing the machine speed and shortening the stitch length, will give you more control while sewing.

- When sewing a curve, always place the convex unit on the bottom and the concave unit on top. With a little manipulation, the curves will line up, then proceed to sew. If possible, set the needle to the needle-down position on the sewing machine. The needle will hold the fabrics in place while you lift the presser foot to make any adjustments. Some machines will lift the presser foot automatically when you stop to adjust your fabric, but this can be done manually as well.

- Even though you may have to slightly stretch and manipulate the concave and convex pieces to line them up, remember that they are the exact same curve at the stitching line and will want to line up. They just need a little coaxing.

Seam Allowance

It is important to use a scant ¼″ seam allowance while piecing curves. A scant ¼″ seam allowance will compensate for the thickness of the thread in the curve, making the two pieces meet perfectly at the stitching line. This keeps the curve nice and smooth and limits distortion of the finished quarter-circle.

It is also important to use a scant ¼″ seam while piecing strips into stripes (see Sewing Stripes, page 21).

Pressing

Pressing curves is no different than pressing straight seams. It is perfectly acceptable to press seams open or to one side or the other.

Pressing a curved seam open will allow the block to lie flatter, but remember that you can't press the seam open if you use glue to baste the curved seam. Choose pins when you want to press the seams open.

There are times when pressing to one side is an advantage. It may be a design choice. If the seam is pressed toward the concave unit, the resulting quarter-circle will look as though it is lying beneath the background. If the seam is pressed toward the convex unit, the quarter-circle will look as though it is sitting on top of the background.

Just as with straight seams, pressing toward the darker fabric will keep dark fabrics from showing beneath light fabrics along the seams of your quilt.

Another reason to press to the side is to reduce seam bulk. Curved piecing, and especially curves that incorporate pieced stripes, can become bulky quickly. Pressing away from pieced stripes is one way to cut down on bulk.

Blending Seams

When you make a quarter-circle with pieced stripes, press the bulky curved seam allowance away from the pieced unit, whether it's concave or convex. When joining 2 quarter-circle squares to make a half-circle, or 4 to make a whole circle, minimizing bulk helps the seams blend to make a smooth curve. Otherwise, the curve can look broken or disjointed.

Pin at each seam where the color changes to help the seams match as you stitch them.

Trimming

Often blocks incorporating curves will need to be squared up. Most premade acrylic templates will have slightly wider outside seam allowances for built-in trimming allowances, but the patterns in this book (and most books and single patterns) do not.

This doesn't mean there isn't opportunity to square or trim the blocks. The best way to maintain the shape of your quarter-circle units is to cut accurate concave and convex units and to baste or pin before sewing.

Because curves are cut on a bias, pressing too aggressively or stretching and pulling on the fabric will contribute to a block being out of square. When squaring a block with no trimming allowance, trim only the portions of the block that are larger than the desired size. This should be enough to square up most blocks.

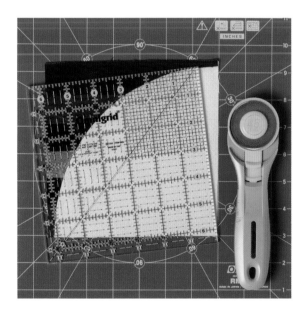

TIP

The best way to prevent having to square up a block is accurately cutting units from the templates.

Making a Quarter-Circle

1. Fold each unit, separately, in half along the curve to find the center. Mark the center either with a fabric marker, finger-pressing, pressing, or pinning.

2. Line up the two pieces right sides together and pin at the center.

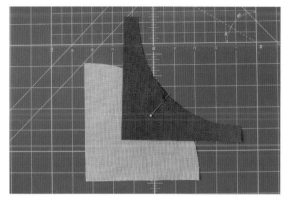

3. If pinning, place pins at both the start and end of the curve. Lining up the straight ends that are perpendicular to the curve will help prevent the curve from warping. Placing pins at these two edges is an option.

4. Pin as needed along the curve, lining up the edges as you go. A general rule of thumb is the smaller the curve, the more pins that will be needed.

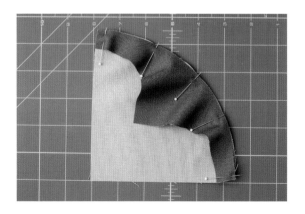

5. If glue basting, apply glue to half the curve of the convex piece, starting at the center. Line up the edges and press the two pieces together to set the glue. Apply glue to the remaining half of the curve. Line up the edges and press the 2 pieces together to set the glue.

6. Sew along the curve with a scant ¼″ seam allowance, removing the pins as you go.

7. Press the seam as desired and square up the block if needed.

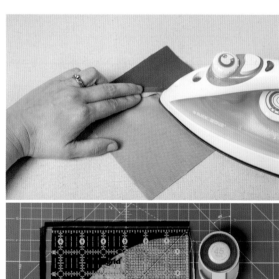

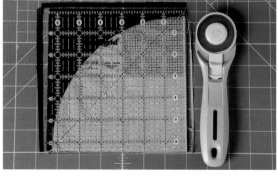

TIP
Curve piecing can be chain-pieced, just like straight piecing!

Double Quarter-Circles

One variation of the quarter-circle block is the double quarter-circle, which adds an arc between the concave and convex units. When 4 of these blocks are pieced together, it will look like a circle with a ring around the outside, or a double circle. All the tips and techniques for a standard quarter-circle unit apply to piecing the double-quarter-circle.

Double quarter-circle

A double quarter-circle unit is made from three pieces: concave, arc, and convex. The concave and convex are exactly the same as the quarter-circle units but the arc piece is what creates the look of layered or concentric circles.

1. Fold the convex piece in half along the curve and mark the center by finger-pressing a crease into the fabric.

2. Fold the arc piece in half along the inside curve and mark the center by finger-pressing a crease into the fabric.

3. Place the pieces right sides together, line up the center creases.

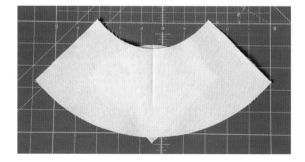

4. Place a pin at the center crease. Line up and pin both ends of the 2 pieces or glue baste the 2 curves together. We recommend you use *a minimum of 3 pins*.

Lining up the straight ends that are perpendicular to the curve will help the curve from warping. Placing pins at these 2 edges is an option.

Line up and pin along the 2 curves as necessary.

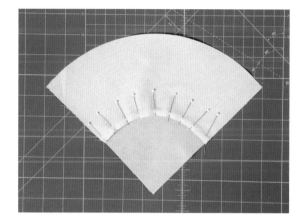

5. Sew the pieces together along the curve using a scant ¼″. Press the seams open to finish a 2-color convex unit.

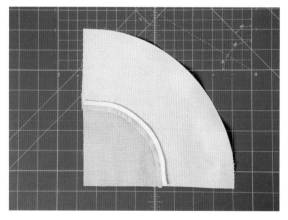

6. Fold the 2-color convex unit in half along the curve and mark the center with a fabric marker, pressing or finger-pressing a crease into the fabric.

7. Fold the concave piece in half along the curve and mark the center with a fabric marker, pressing or finger-pressing a crease into the fabric.

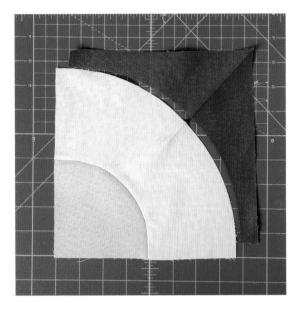

8. Pin at both the start and end of the curve. Lining up the straight ends that are perpendicular to the curve will help the curve from warping. Placing pins at these two edges is an option.

Pin as needed along the curve, lining up the edges as you go. A general rule of thumb is the smaller the curve the more pins will be need.

If glue basting, glue along the curve and line up the curves. You may need to press the two pieces together to set the glue.

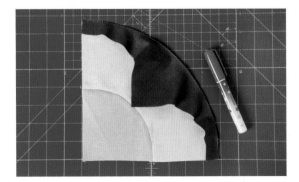

9. Sew along the curve with a scant ¼˝ seam allowance removing the pins, if any, as you go.

10. Press the seam as desired and square if needed.

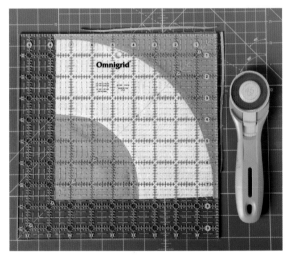

SEWING STRIPES

There are few tips and tricks to making strips of fabrics into even and uniform stripes.

- Test your seam allowance. You can do this by sewing 2 strips both 1½″ in width together. The resulting strip should be 2½″ in width. If it isn't 2½″, double check that you are using a scant ¼″ to account for the thickness of the thread. Adjust your seam allowance until the desired result is reached.

- To keep the strip set from bowing in the middle, change the direction you sew from at the beginning of each strip. If the strip set is made up of only 2 colors, you can accomplish this by always keeping the same color on top. If there are multiple colors in the strip set, it can be more difficult, but this rule still applies with a slight alteration—keep the same color on top while working with that color.

- Press the strip set with a starch or nonstarch alternative, such as Flatter (by Soak). This will help the stripes lie flat. You can also straighten stripes by manipulating the fabric while pressing.

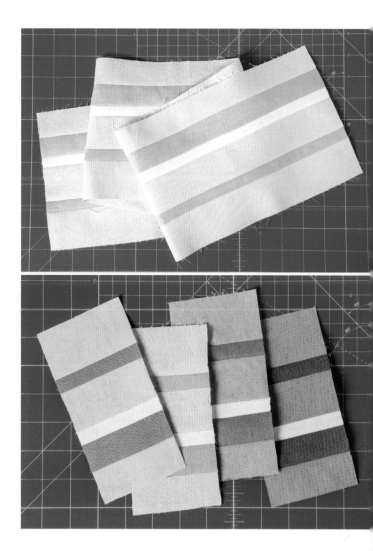

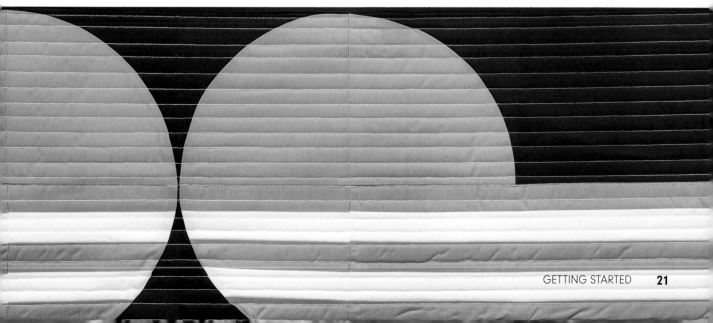

RETRO SPIN

FINISHED BLOCK: 10″ × 10″ • FINISHED QUILT: 60″ × 72″

Retro Spin is a modern sampler that uses repeating blocks to keep the design uniform and clean. The rotating blocks create movement and the stripes add depth.

MATERIALS

Yardages are based on 40″ usable width. (Fabrics in parentheses are by Robert Kaufman Fabrics.)

Fabric

CREAM *(Kona Bone)*: 1 yard

PALE PINK *(Kona Lingerie)*: 2 yards for background

LIGHT PINK *(Kona Doe Skin)*: 1⅜ yards for outer border

DARK GRAY *(Kona Charcoal)*: ½ yard

LIGHT GRAY *(Kona Overcast)*: ⅔ yard

ORANGE *(Kona Tangerine)*: ½ yard

AQUA *(Kona Dusty Blue)*: ½ yard

YELLOW *(Kona Curry)*: ½ yard

DARK YELLOW *(Kona Yarrow)*: ½ yard

LIGHT GREEN *(Kona Leaf)*: ⅓ yard

GREEN *(Kona Palm)*: ½ yard

DARK GREEN *(Kona Pesto)*: ⅓ yard

BINDING: ⅝ yard

BACKING: 4½ yards

Other materials

BATTING: 68″ × 80″

TEMPLATES: Make templates from these patterns:
5″ Concave (page 125)
and 5″ Convex (page 124).

TIP

If you'd like to use a printed stripe fabric instead of piecing the stripes, see Printed Stripe Option (page 29).

CUTTING

See Cutting Techniques (page 13) for more information about how to cut curves and use fabric efficiently.
See the cutting diagrams for concave and convex pieces (page 14).

FABRIC	CUT	SUBCUT		
		Rectangles, squares, and strips	5″ concave ⌐	5″ convex ◠
Cream	1 strip 5½″ × WOF*			5
	4 strips 2½″ × WOF	1 strip 2½″ × 34½″ 2 strips 2½″ × 26½″ 1 strip 2½″ × 25½″ 10 rectangles 2½″ × 5½″		
	5 strips 2″ × WOF	20 rectangles 2″ × 5½″		
	4 strips 1½″ × WOF	1 strip 1½″ × 34½″ 2 strips 1½″ × 26½″ 1 strip 1½″ × 25½″		
Pale pink	14 strips 2½″ × WOF	1 strip 2½″ × 34½″ 1 strip 2½″ × 26½″ 5 strips 2½″ × 24½″ 5 strips 2½″ × 22½″ 15 rectangles 2½″ × 10½		
	5 strips 5½″ × WOF		20	20
Light pink	4 strips 6½″ × WOF	1 strip 6½″ × 35½″ 2 strips 6½″ × 30½″ 1 strip 6½″ × 28½″		
	4 strips 3½″ × WOF	1 strip 3½″ × 35½″ 2 strips 3½″ × 30½″ 1 strip 3½″ × 28½″		
Dark gray	2 strips 5½″ × WOF			15
Light gray	2 strips 2½″ × WOF	10 rectangles 2½″ × 5½″		
	5 strips 2″ × WOF	20 rectangles 2″ × 5½″		
Orange	2 strips 5½″ × WOF		20	
Aqua	2 strips 5½″ × WOF		20	
Yellow	2 strips 3½″ × WOF	10 rectangles 3½″ × 5½″		
	2 strips 2½″ × WOF	10 rectangles 2½″ × 5½″		

FABRIC	CUT	SUBCUT		
		Rectangles, squares, and strips	5″ concave ◿	5″ convex ◺
Dark yellow	2 strips 3½″ × WOF	10 rectangles 3½″ × 5½″		
	2 strips 2½″ × WOF	10 rectangles 2½″ × 5½″		
Light green	1 strip 5½″ × WOF			5
Green	2 strips 5½″ × WOF			10
Dark green	1 strip 5½″ × WOF			5

WOF = width of fabric

Retro Spin, 60″ × 72″; designed, pieced, and quilted by Heather Black; 2018

CONSTRUCTION

See Piecing Basics (page 15) for more details about how to sew, press, and trim the curves and stripes for this quilt.

Block A

1. Make the following quarter-circles:

   - 1 orange concave / cream convex

   - 3 orange concave / dark gray convex

2. Arrange the units to form a circle. Sew the units together in pairs, then join the pairs to complete the block.

3. Repeat to make 5 blocks total.

Block A. Make 5.

Block B

1. Using the 2½˝ × 5½˝ and 2˝ × 5½˝ rectangles, make the following striped-square units, with the taller rectangle in the middle:

   - 2 cream / light gray / cream

   - 2 light gray / cream / light gray

2. Referring to the Block B cutting diagram, arrange the squares to form a large striped square.

3. Cut 4 convex pieces using the 5˝ convex template.

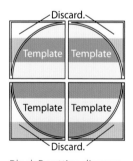

Block B cutting diagram

4. Sew an aqua concave piece to each striped convex piece.

5. Arrange the units to form a circle, with the stripes in the same positions they were in the original square. Sew the units together in pairs, then join the pairs to complete the block.

6. Repeat to make 5 blocks total.

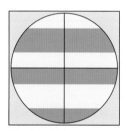

Block B. Make 5.

Block C

1. Make the following quarter-circles:

- 2 pale pink concave / green convex
- 1 pale pink concave / light green convex
- 1 pale pink concave / dark green convex

2. Arrange the units to form a circle. Sew the units together in pairs, then join the pairs to complete the block.

3. Repeat to make 5 blocks total.

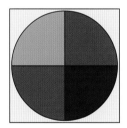

Block C. Make 5.

Block D

1. Using the 3½″ × 5½″ and 2½″ × 5½″ rectangles, make the following striped squares:

- 2 yellow 3½″ × 5½″ / dark yellow 2½″ × 5½″
- 2 yellow 2½″ × 5½″ / dark yellow 3½″ × 5½″

2. Referring to the Block D cutting diagram, arrange the squares to form a large striped square.

3. Cut 4 concave pieces using the 5″ concave template.

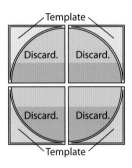

4. Sew a pale pink convex piece to each striped concave unit.

5. Arrange the units to form a circle, with the stripes in the same positions they were in the original square. Sew the units together in pairs, then join the pairs to complete the block.

6. Repeat to make 5 blocks total.

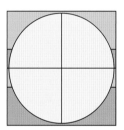

Block D. Make 5.

Sashing and Borders

Sashing

Sew end-to-end pale pink strips 2½″ × 24½″ and 2½″ × 22½″ to make a 2½″ × 46½″ strip. Make 5.

Inner Borders

1. Sew end-to-end pale pink strips 2½″ × 34½″ and 2½″ × 26½″ to make a 2½″ × 60½″ strip for the right inner border.

2. Sew the following cream strips end to end:

   • 2½″ × 26½″ and 2½″ × 34½″ to make a 2½″ × 60½″ strip for the right inner border

   • 1½″ × 25½″ and 1½″ × 26½″ to make a 1½″ × 51½″ strip for the top inner border

   • 2½″ × 25½″ and 2½″ × 26½″ to make a 2½″ × 51½″ strip for the bottom inner border

   • 1½″ × 26½″ and 1½″ × 34½″ to make a 1½″ × 60½″ strip for the left inner border

Outer Border

Sew the following light pink strips end to end:

   • 2 strips 3½″ × 30½″ to make a 3½″ × 60½″ strip for the top border

   • 2 strips 6½″ × 30½″ to make a 6½″ × 60½″ strip for the bottom border

   • 3½″ × 28½″ and 3½″ × 35½″ to make a 3½″ × 63½″ strip for the left border

   • 6½″ × 28½″ and 6½″ × 35½″ to make a 6½″ × 63½″ strip for the right border

Quilt Assembly

Refer to the quilt assembly diagram (next page).

1. Sew the blocks and pale pink 2½″ × 10½″ sashing strips into rows.

2. Sew the rows and horizontal pale pink sashing strips together.

3. Sew the pale pink and cream right and cream left inner borders to the quilt body.

4. Sew the top and bottom inner borders to the quilt body.

5. Sew the right and left outer borders to the quilt body.

6. Sew the top and bottom outer borders to the quilt body to complete the top.

Finishing

Layer, quilt, and bind as desired.

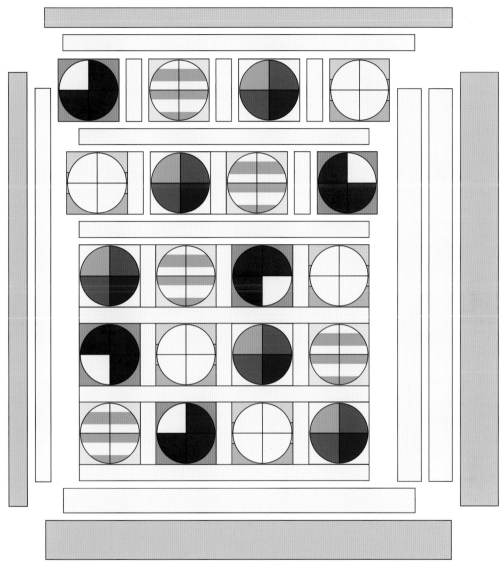

Quilt assembly

PRINTED STRIPE OPTION

If you want to use a printed stripe instead of the strip units:

- Purchase ⅔ yard of a high-contrast stripe for the cream and light gray 5½″ convex pieces and ½ yard low-contrast stripe for the 5½″ yellow and dark yellow concave pieces.

- Cut 3 high-contrast stripe strips 5½″ × width of fabric; subcut 20 convex pieces with the 5½″ convex template.

- Cut 2 low-contrast stripe strips 5½″ × width of fabric; subcut 20 concave pieces with the 5½″ concave template.

LYS

FINISHED QUILT: 48″ × 70″

In Norwegian, the word for "light" is *lys*. During the time I've lived in Norway, I've been acutely aware of light throughout all the seasons. In the summer, the light persists to create long, lingering days. In the winter, sunlight appears for a short time each day, but just as with most Scandinavian countries, people here weave light into the winter months with candles and paper star lanterns. *Lys* celebrates all of the different varieties of light.

MATERIALS

Yardages are based on 40″ usable width. (Fabrics in parentheses are by Robert Kaufman Fabrics.)

Fabric

YELLOW 1 A *(Kona Lemon)*: ⅓ yard

YELLOW 2 A *(Kona Daffodil)*: ⅓ yard

YELLOW 3 B *(Kona Sunflower)*: ⅓ yard

YELLOW 4 B *(Kona Sunny)*: ⅓ yard

YELLOW 5 B *(Kona Grellow)*: ⅓ yard

YELLOW 6 B *(Kona Buttercup)*: ⅓ yard

YELLOW 7 B *(Kona Citrus)*: ⅓ yard

YELLOW 8 B *(Kona Corn Yellow)*: ⅓ yard

BLUE *(Kona Blue Jay)*: 2½ yards

YELLOW *(Kona Canary)*: ⅔ yard for binding

BACKING: 3¼ yards

Other materials

BATTING: 56″ × 78″

TEMPLATES: Make templates from these patterns: 3″ Concave (page 125) and 3″ Convex (page 122).

CUTTING

See Cutting Techniques (page 13) for more information about how to cut curves and use fabric efficiently. See the cutting diagrams for concave and convex pieces (page 14).

FABRIC	CUT	SUBCUT		
		Rectangles, squares, and strips	3″ concave	3″ convex
"A" yellows	**From *each* of the 2 yellows, cut:**			
	1 strip 3½″ × WOF* (2 total)	1 rectangle 3½″ × 15½″ (2 total)	6 (12 total)	
	1 strip 3½″ × WOF (2 total)			8 (16 total)
"B" yellows	**From *each* of the 6 yellows, cut:**			
	1 strip 3½″ × WOF (6 total)	1 rectangle 3½″ × 27½″ (6 total)	2 (12 total)	
	1 strip 3½″ × WOF (6 total)	1 rectangle 3½″ × 15½″ (6 total)		4 (24 total)
Blue	5 strips 3½″ × WOF		40	24
	2 strips 23½″ × WOF	**From *each* strip, subcut:** 1 rectangle 23½″ × 27½″ (2 total) 1 rectangle 21½″ × 8½″ (2 total)		
	1 strip 9½″ × WOF	2 rectangles 9½″ × 15½″		

* WOF = width of fabric

CONSTRUCTION

See Piecing Basics (page 15) for more details about how to sew, press, and trim the curves for this quilt.

Fabrics with little contrast work well in this pattern, but when using a monochromatic palette, label well for organization and efficient sewing.

1. Make 40 quarter-circles:

• blue concave / yellow convex

2. Matching the yellow fabrics, sew the quarter-circles into pairs to make 20 yellow half-circles.

3. Make 24 quarter-circles:

• "A" yellow concave / blue convex

4. Matching the yellow fabrics, sew the quarter-circles in pairs to create 12 half-circles.

5. Match 2 half-circles from Step 4 with "A" yellow concave pieces to make a full circle. Make 3.

Lys, 48″ × 70″; designed, pieced, and quilted by Daisy Aschehoug; 2018

Quilt Assembly

Refer to the quilt assembly diagram (next page).

1. Choose a layout for the yellow "B" rectangles by following the quilt assembly diagram. Arrange the half-circles from Construction, Step 4 (page 32), to match up with the yellow rectangles.

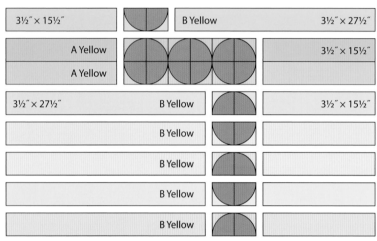

3½" × 15½"		B Yellow	3½" × 27½"
A Yellow			3½" × 15½"
A Yellow			
3½" × 27½"		B Yellow	3½" × 15½"
		B Yellow	
		B Yellow	
		B Yellow	
		B Yellow	

Determine the order of yellows, then arrange the blue half-circles so the yellow edges match the yellow in the row.

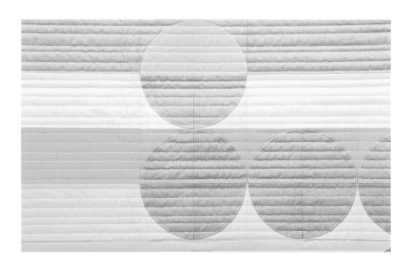

2. Sew the half-circles together to make full circles.

3. Arrange the full circles and half-circles together with the background strips as shown.

4. Sew each row together, then join the rows.

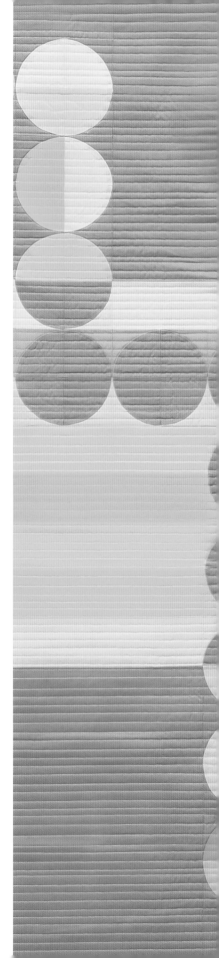

Finishing

Layer, quilt, and bind as desired.

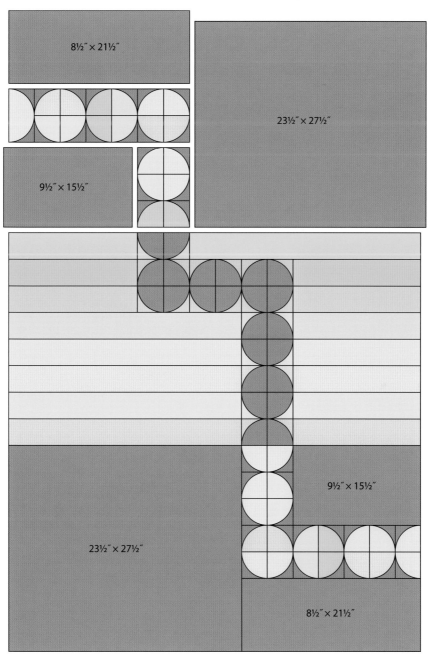

Quilt assembly

PERFECT DOZEN

FINISHED BLOCK: 12″ × 12″ • FINISHED QUILT: 60″ × 72″

Perfect Dozen is a perfectly modern way to display curves and stripes. This design has it all—pieced and printed stripes, stripes in the background, stripes in the foreground, stripes in the borders, and not to mention twelve full circles! The simplicity of this quilt doesn't lack any impact.

MATERIALS

Yardages are based on 40″ usable width. (Fabrics in parentheses are by Robert Kaufman Fabrics.)

Fabric

CHECK *("Out of Print" Grey)*: 3⅞ yards

BROWN *(Crawford Stripes Brown)*: ½ yard

GREEN *(Crawford Stripes Forest)*: ⅓ yard

PINK *(Kona Pearl Pink)*: ⅝ yard

RED *(Kona Paprika)*: ⅜ yard

AQUA *(Kona Seafoam)*: ½ yard

GRAY *(Kona Overcast)*: ⅝ yard

BINDING: ⅝ yard

BACKING: 4½ yards

Other materials

BATTING: 68″ × 80″ (I used Warm & Natural by The Warm Company.)

TEMPLATES: Make templates from these patterns: 6″ Concave with 1″ Float (page 125) and 5″ Convex (page 124).

TIP

If you'd like to use a printed stripe fabric instead of piecing the stripes, see Printed Stripe Option (page 43).

CUTTING

See Cutting Techniques (page 13) for more information about how to cut curves and use fabric efficiently.
See the cutting diagrams for concave and convex pieces (page 14).

FABRIC	CUT	SUBCUT		
		Rectangles, squares, and strips	6″ concave with 1″ float	5″ convex
Check	2 strips 18½″ × WOF*	2 strips 18½″ × 30½″		
	2 strips 12½″ × WOF	2 strips 12½″ × 36½″		
	5 strips 6½″ × WOF	2 strips 6½″ × 30½″	26	
	1 strip 5½″ × WOF			8
	3 strips 4″ × WOF	4 rectangles 4″ × 12½″ 8 rectangles 4″ × 6½″		
	3 strips 1½″ × WOF	4 rectangles 1½″ × 12½″ 8 rectangles 1½″ × 6½″		
Brown	1 strip 6½″ × WOF		4	4
	2 strips 1½″ × WOF	8 rectangles 1½″ × 6½″		
Green	1 strip 5½″ × WOF			4
	1 strip 1½″ × WOF	4 rectangles 1½″ × 6½″		
	1 strip 1″ × WOF	4 rectangles 1″ × 6½″		
Pink	1 strip 6½″ × WOF	4 rectangles 6½″ × 2½″ 4 rectangles 6½″ × 2″	2	
	2 strips 5½″ × WOF			12
Red	1 strip 5½″ × WOF			8
	1 strip 1½″ × WOF	4 rectangles 1½″ × 6½″		
	1 strip 1″ × WOF	4 rectangles 1″ × 6½″		
Aqua	1 strip 5½″ × WOF			8
	1 strip 2″ × WOF	4 rectangles 2″ × 6½″		
	1 strip 1½″ × WOF	4 rectangles 1½″ × 6½″		
Gray	1 strip 5½″ × WOF			4
	4 strips 1½″ × WOF	6 rectangles 1½″ × 12½″ 12 rectangles 1½″ × 6½″		
	2 strips 1″ × WOF	8 rectangles 1″ × 6½″		

* WOF = width of fabric

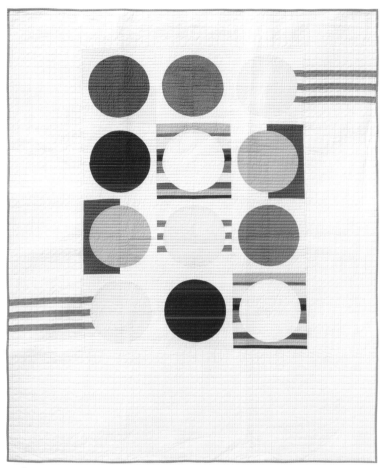

Perfect Dozen, 60″ × 72″; designed, pieced, and quilted by Heather Black; 2018

CONSTRUCTION

See Piecing Basics (page 15) for more details about how to sew, press, and trim the curves and stripes for this quilt.

TIP

Lay out all blocks in the proper orientation before cutting templates and/or piecing. This will help prevent piecing stripes in the wrong direction.

Block A

1. Make the following quarter-circles:

- 2 pink concave / brown convex

- 2 check concave / brown convex

2. Arrange the units to form a circle as shown. Sew the units in pairs, then join the pairs to complete the block.

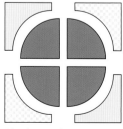

Block A. Make 1.

Block B

1. Make the following quarter-circles:

- 4 check concave / green convex

2. Arrange the units to form a circle. Sew the units together in pairs, then join the pairs to complete the block.

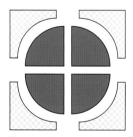

Block B. Make 1.

Block C

1. Make the following quarter-circles:

   • 2 check concave /
     pink convex

2. Sew the units from Step 1 together to make a half-circle.

3. Sew the following rectangles together to make a striped square:

   • check 4″ × 6½″

   • gray 1½″ × 6½″

   • check 1½″ × 6½″

   • gray 1″ × 6½″

   Make 2.

4. Cut a concave piece from each striped square using the 6″ concave with 1″ float template. Refer to the block diagram to see how to position the concave template with the stripes.

5. Make the following quarter-circles, using the concave pieces from Step 4:

   • 2 striped concave /
     pink convex

6. Sew the units from Step 5 together to make a half-circle unit.

7. Join the half-circles from Steps 2 and 6 to complete the block.

8. Repeat to make 2 blocks total.

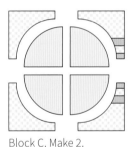

Block C. Make 2.

Block D

1. Make the following quarter-circles:

   • 4 check concave /
     red convex

2. Arrange the units to form a circle. Sew the units together in pairs, then join the pairs to complete the block.

3. Repeat to make 2 blocks total.

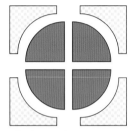

Block D. Make 2.

Block E

1. Sew the following rectangles in order to make a 6½″ striped square:

   • aqua 2″ × 6½″

   • green 1″ × 6½″

   • pink 2½″ × 6½″

   • brown 1½″ × 6½″

   • red 1½″ × 6½″

2. Repeat to make 2 total.

3. Sew the following rectangles in order to make a 6½″ striped square:

   • gray 1½″ × 6½″

   • green 1½″ × 6½″

   • pink 2″ × 6½″

   • brown 1½″ × 6½″

   • aqua 1½″ × 6½″

   • red 1″ × 6½″

4. Repeat to make 2 total.

5. Arrange the squares as shown in the block diagram. Cut a concave piece from each square using the 6″ concave with 1″ float template. Take care to orient the direction of the concave unit according to the block diagram.

6. Sew a check convex piece to each of the striped concave pieces from Step 5.

7. Arrange the units to form a circle, matching stripes. Sew the units together in pairs, then join the pairs to complete the block.

8. Repeat to make 2 blocks total.

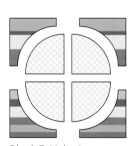

Block E. Make 2.

Block F

1. Make the following quarter-circles:

   • 2 brown concave / aqua convex

   • 2 check concave / aqua convex

2. Arrange the units to form a circle. Sew the units together in pairs, then join the pairs to complete the block.

3. Repeat to make 2 blocks total.

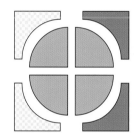

Block F. Make 2.

Block G

1. Sew the following rectangles together to make a striped 6½″ square:

   • check 4″ × 6½″

   • gray 1½″ × 6½″

   • check 1½″ × 6½″

   • gray 1″ × 6½″

   Make 4.

2. Cut a concave piece from each striped square using the 6″ concave with 1″ float template. Refer to the block G diagram (at right) to see how to position the concave template with the stripes.

3. Make the following quarter-circles, using the concave pieces from Step 2:

   • 4 striped concave / pink convex

4. Arrange the units to form a circle as shown. Sew the units in pairs, then join the pairs to complete the block.

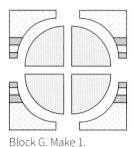

Block G. Make 1.

Block H

1. Make the following quarter-circles:

   • 4 check concave / gray convex

2. Arrange the units to form a circle as shown. Sew the units in pairs, then join the pairs to complete the block.

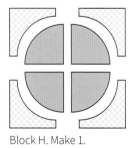

Block H. Make 1.

Block I

1. Sew the following rectangles to make a striped 12½″ square.

   • check 4″ × 12½″

   • gray 1½″ × 12½″

   • check 1½″ × 12½″

   • gray 1½″ × 12½″

   • check 1½″ × 12½″

   • gray 1½″ × 12½″

   • check 4″ × 12½″

2. Repeat to make 2 blocks total.

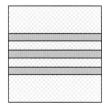

Block I. Make 2.

Sashing and Borders

1. Sew the following checked strips end to end:

   • 2 strips 6½″ × 30½″ to make a top border strip 6½″ × 60½″

   • 2 strips 18½″ × 30½″ to make a bottom border strip 18½″ × 60½″

2. Sew a Block I to the end of a check strip 12½″ × 36½″ to make a left border strip 12½″ × 48½″. Repeat for the right border.

Quilt Assembly

Refer to the quilt assembly diagram.

1. Sew the blocks into rows.

2. Sew the rows together.

3. Sew the right and left borders to the quilt body, matching the gray stripes.

4. Sew the top and bottom borders to the quilt body to complete the quilt top.

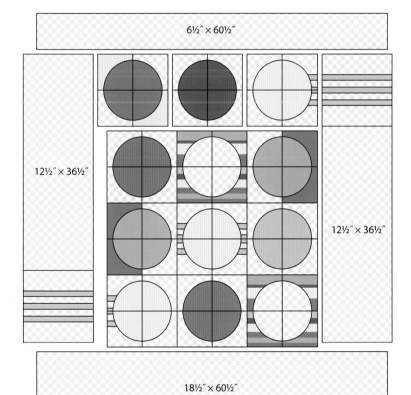

Quilt assembly

Finishing

Layer, quilt, and bind as desired.

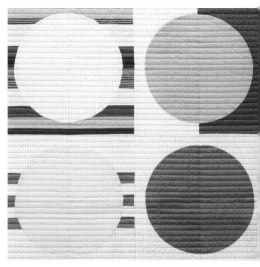

PRINTED STRIPE OPTION

If you want to use a printed stripe, purchase ⅜ yard of a multistripe and ⅓ yard of a bicolor strip. Cut 8 multistripe concave units using the 6½˝ concave with 1˝ border template. Cut 2 bicolor rectangles 4˝ × 12½˝ and 8 bicolor rectangles 3½˝ × 6½˝ (fussy cutting stripes may be necessary).

BEACH DAY

FINISHED QUILT: 52″ × 63″

Beach Day is inspired by the sun rising and setting on the horizon beyond a waterfront. A tricolor palette conjures up a retro look, hinting at a cool 70's beach towel.

MATERIALS

Yardages are based on 40″ usable width. (Fabrics in parentheses are by Robert Kaufman Fabrics.)

Fabric

WHITE *(Kona White)*: ⅝ yard

PINK *(Kona Rose)*:

  1½ yards for piecing

  ⅔ yard for binding

BLUE *(Kona Windsor)*: 1½ yards

BACKING: 3⅓ yards

Other materials

BATTING: 60″ × 71″

TEMPLATES: Make templates from these patterns:
6″ Concave (page 124) and
6″ Convex (page 122).

CUTTING

See Cutting Techniques (page 13) for more information about how to cut curves and use fabric efficiently. See the cutting diagrams for concave and convex pieces (page 14).

FABRIC	CUT	SUBCUT		
		Rectangles, squares, and strips	6″ concave	6″ convex
White	18 strips 1½″ × WOF*			
Pink	18 strips 1½″ × WOF			
	3 strips 6½″ × WOF			16
Blue	5 strips 3½″ × WOF			
	2 strips 3½″ × WOF	5 rectangles 3½″ × 12½″		
	4 strips 6½″ × WOF	8 rectangles 6½″ × 14½″		
	3 strips 6½″ × WOF		24	

* *WOF = width of fabric*

CONSTRUCTION

See Piecing Basics (page 15) for more details about how to sew, press, and trim the curves and stripes for this quilt.

Strip Sets

1. Sew 3 pink 1½˝ strips and 3 white 1½˝ strips together, alternating the colors.

2. Repeat to make 6 total.

3. From 4 strip sets, subcut 8 rectangles 6½˝ × 20½˝.

4. From the remaining 2 strip sets, subcut 8 convex pieces using the 6˝ convex template.

Be sure strip sets are oriented correctly when cutting convex curves.

Striped Quarter-Circles

1. Make the following quarter-circles:

   • 8 blue concave / pink stripe convex

Blue/Pink Half-Circles

1. Make the following quarter-circles:

   • 16 blue concave / pink convex

2. Sew the quarter-circles together in pairs to make 8 half-circles.

Row Assembly

1. Sew each blue/pink half-circle to a blue 6½˝ × 14½˝ rectangle, sewing 4 half-circles to the right end of the rectangle and 4 to the left.

2. Sew each striped quarter-circle to a striped 6½˝ × 20½˝ rectangle, sewing 4 half-circles to the right end of the rectangle and 4 to the left. Match the stripes across the seams.

3. Sew the units together to make 4 rows.

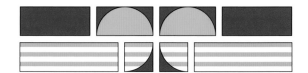

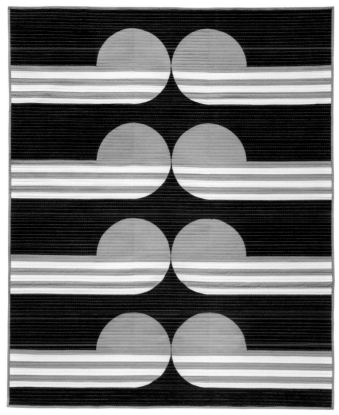

Beach Day, 52″ × 63″; designed, pieced, and quilted by Daisy Aschehoug; 2018

Quilt Assembly

Refer to the quilt assembly diagram.

1. Sew end-to-end a blue 3½″ × 13″ rectangle and a blue 3½″ × 40″ rectangle to make a strip 3½″ × 52½″ for horizontal sashing. Make 5.

2. Arrange the sashings and rows together, beginning with sashing at the top.

3. Sew the sashing and rows together to complete the top.

Finishing

Layer, quilt, and bind as desired.

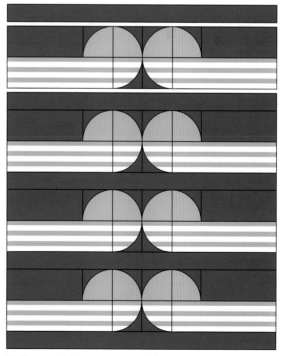

Quilt assembly

DANCING CUPS

FINISHED QUILT: 47˝ × 54˝

Dancing Cups echoes the idea of farmhouse bowls stacked in a classic blue and white kitchen.

MATERIALS

Yardages are based on 40˝ usable width. (Fabrics in parentheses are by Robert Kaufman Fabrics.)

Fabric

GRAY *(Kona Shadow)*: 3 yards

BLUE *(Kona Windsor)*:

⅝ yard for piecing

½ yard for binding

BACKING: 3⅛ yards

Other materials

BATTING: 55˝ × 62˝

TEMPLATES: Make templates from these patterns:
3˝ Concave (page 125) and
3˝ Convex (page 122).

CUTTING

See Cutting Techniques (page 13) for more information about how to cut curves and use fabric efficiently. See the cutting diagrams for concave and convex pieces (page 14).

FABRIC	CUT	SUBCUT		
		Rectangles, squares, and strips	3˝ concave	3˝ convex
Gray	32 strips 1½˝ × WOF*			
	3 strips 6⅞˝ × WOF	15 squares 6⅞˝ × 6⅞˝ **		
	1 strip 7¼˝ × WOF	2 squares 7¼˝ × 7¼˝ ** 2 squares 5˝ × 5˝ **		
	3 strips 3½˝ × WOF		48	
	2 strips 3⅞˝ × WOF	12 squares 3⅞˝ × 3⅞˝ **		
Blue	24 strips 1½˝ × WOF			
	5 strips 3½˝ × WOF			48

* WOF = width of fabric
** Cut each square on the diagonal to make 2 triangles. Handle these triangles carefully so as not to stretch the bias edges.

CONSTRUCTION

See Piecing Basics (page 15) for more details about how to sew, press, and trim the curves and stripes for this quilt.

Dancing Cups Blocks

Half-Circles

1. Make the following quarter-circles:

   • 48 gray concave / blue convex

2. Sew the units together in pairs to make 24 half-circles.

Block A

1. Referring to the block diagram, sew a 3⅞″ triangle and a 6⅞″ triangle to a half-circle as shown. Press gently so as not to distort the bias edges.

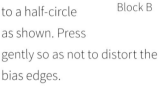

Block A

2. Repeat to make 12 total.

Block B

1. Referring to the block diagram, sew a 3⅞″ triangle and a 6⅞″ triangle to a half-circle as shown. Press gently so as not to distort the bias edges.

3⅞″

6⅞″

Block B

2. Repeat to make 12 total.

Cup Columns

1. Referring to the column assembly diagram and starting at the top of the column, sew a 7¼″ triangle to the cup edge of Block A.

2. Sew a Block B to the other diagonal edge of Block A.

3. Continue to join blocks, alternating Block A and Block B until the column has 8 blocks, 4 of each.

4. Sew a 5″ triangle to the bottom right edge to complete the row.

5. Repeat to create 3 columns total. Trim each column to 54½″.

Column assembly

Pieced Stripe Columns

1. Using the 1½″ strips, make the following strip sets:

   • 2: gray / blue / gray / blue / gray / blue / gray

2. Join the strip sets and trim to make a column 7½″ × 54½″.

3. Repeat to make 4 total.

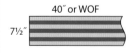

40″ or WOF

7½″

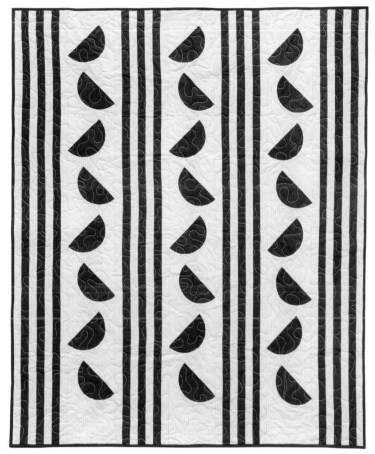

Dancing Cups, 47″ × 54″; designed, pieced, and quilted by Daisy Aschehoug; 2018

Quilt Assembly

Refer to the quilt assembly diagram.

1. Sew a cup column to the left side of 3 of the striped columns.

2. Sew the columns together.

3. Sew the last striped column to the left side of the first cup column to complete the quilt top.

Finishing

Layer, quilt, and bind as desired.

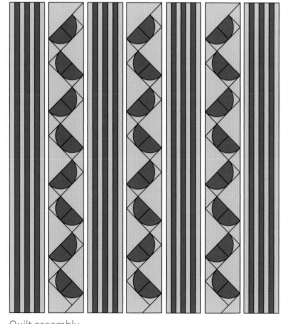

Quilt assembly

FINS

FINISHED QUILT: 48″ × 60″

Fins uses unexpected curves to break up a bold arrangement of lines.

MATERIALS

Yardages are based on 40″ usable width. (Fabrics in parentheses are by Robert Kaufman Fabrics.)

Fabric

WHITE *(Kona White)*: 1 yard

LIGHT ORANGE *(Kona Coral)*: ½ yard

DARK ORANGE *(Kona Persimmon)*: 1 fat eighth

LIGHT GREEN *(Kona Clover)*: 1½ yards

DARK GREEN *(Kona Pesto)*:

 1½ yards for piecing

 ½ yard for binding

BACKING: 3⅛ yards

Other materials

BATTING: 56″ × 66″

TEMPLATES: Make templates from these patterns: 6″ Concave (page 124) and 6″ Convex (page 122).

TIP

If you'd like to use a printed stripe fabric instead of piecing the stripes, see Printed Stripe Option (page 59).

CUTTING

See Cutting Techniques (page 13) for more information about how to cut curves and use fabric efficiently. See the cutting diagrams for concave and convex pieces (page 14).

FABRIC	CUT	SUBCUT		
		Rectangles, squares, and strips	6″ concave	6″ convex
White	12 strips 1½″ × WOF*			
	1 strip 6½″ × WOF	1 rectangle 6½″ × 30½″	1	
	1 strip 6½″ × WOF	1 rectangle 6½″ × 12½″		
Orange	2 strips 6½″ × WOF			10
Dark orange				1
Light green	18 strips 1½″ × WOF			
	2 strips 6½″ × WOF	2 rectangles 6½″ × 24½″	2	
	1 strip 6½″ × WOF	2 rectangles 6½″ × 18½″		
Dark green	18 strips 1½″ × WOF			
	1 strip 6½″ × WOF	1 rectangle 6½″ × 30½″		
	1 strip 6½″ × WOF	1 rectangle 6½″ × 12½″ 1 rectangle 6½″ × 9″	1	
	1 strip 6½″ × WOF	1 strip 6½″ × 40″		

* WOF = width of fabric

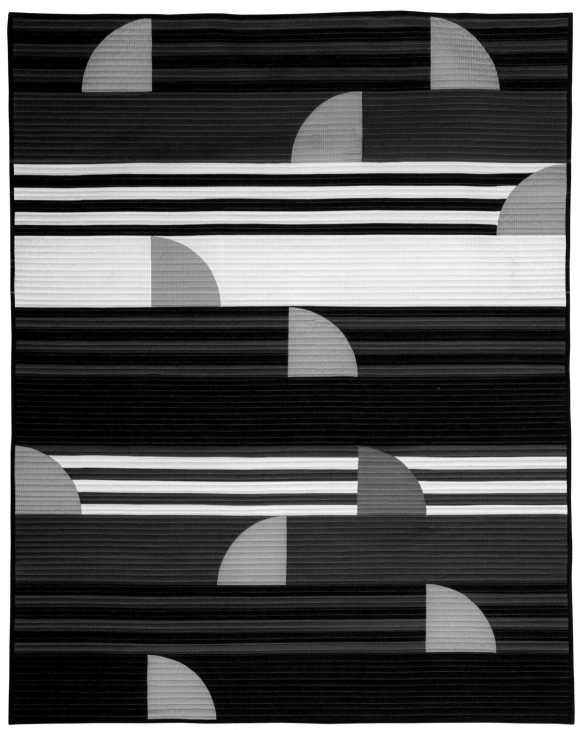

Fins, 48″ × 60″; designed, pieced, and quilted by Daisy Aschehoug; 2018

CONSTRUCTION

See Piecing Basics (page 15) for more details about how to sew, press, and trim the curves and stripes for this quilt.

Strip Sets

Using the 1½″ strips, make the following 6½″ strip sets:

• 2 sets of 3 white / light green, alternating colors

Subcut 1 rectangle 6½″ × 24½″, 1 rectangle 6½″ × 12½″, and 2 concave pieces.

Cut 2 concave pieces with light green strip on horizontal edge.

• 2 sets of 3 white / dark green, alternating colors

Subcut 1 strip 6½″ × 30½″, 1 rectangle 6½″ × 12½″, and 1 concave piece.

Cut 1 concave piece with white strip on horizontal edge.

• 4 sets of 3 light green / dark green, alternating colors

Subcut 1 strip 6½″ × 36½″, 2 strips 6½″ × 24½″, 1 rectangle 6½″ × 18½″, 3 squares 6½″ × 6½″, and 4 concave pieces. Cut a long strip or rectangle from each strip first, then the squares, then the concave pieces.

Cut 1 concave piece with light green strip on horizontal edge.

Cut 1 concave piece with light green strip on horizontal edge.

Cut 2 concave pieces with dark green strips on horizontal edge.

Quarter-Circles

Make the following quarter-circles:

- 1 white and light green concave /
  dark orange convex

- 1 white concave / orange convex

- 2 light green concave / orange convex

- 1 dark green concave / orange convex

- 4 dark and light green striped concave /
  orange convex

- 1 dark green and white concave / orange convex

- 1 white and light green concave / orange convex

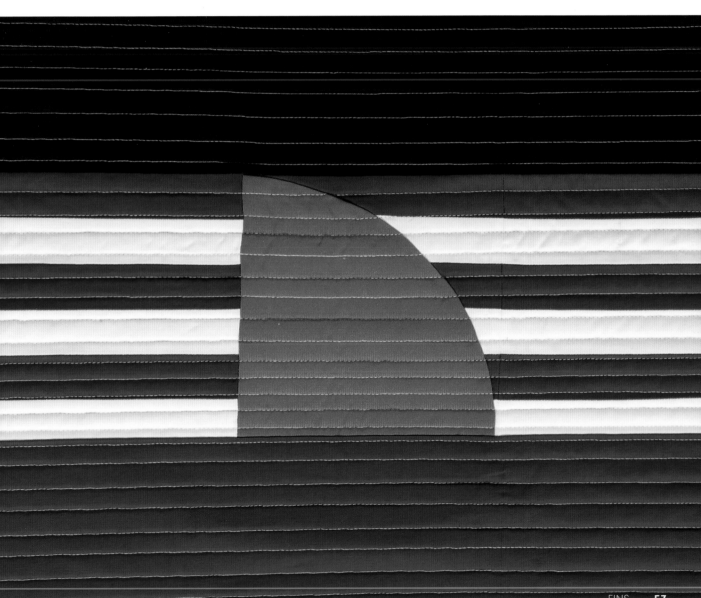

Quilt Assembly

Refer to the quilt assembly diagram.

1. Arrange the quarter-circles and striped and solid units as shown.

2. Sew the units together in rows.

3. Sew the rows together to complete the quilt top.

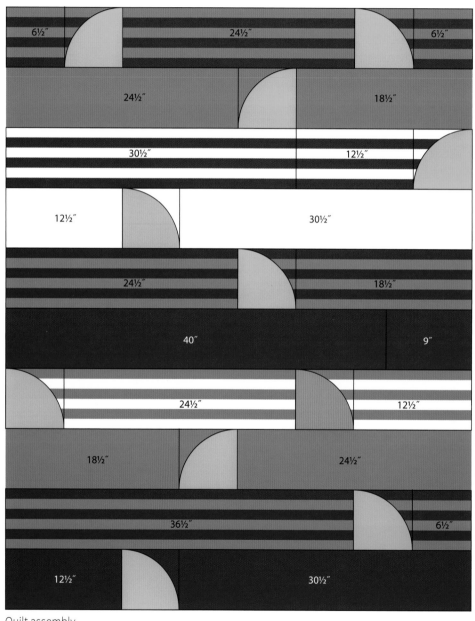

Quilt assembly

PRINTED STRIPE OPTION

If you want to use printed stripes, buy ½ yard of 5 different striped fabrics and 1¾ yards of background fabric.

Substitute the striped fabrics for the strip sets and cut 1 convex piece from each of 4 of the stripes. See the quilt assembly diagram (below right).

From the background fabric, cut all the rectangles, squares, and strips in the cutting chart for the pieced-stripe quilt, except the 1½″ strips.

In my *Fins* variation, the thin stripes run vertically in each row instead of in long horizontal lines as in the original pieced-strips quilt. That's because I ordered the fabric thinking that the stripes ran from selvage to selvage. Instead, they were perpendicular to the selvage, so I ended up with vertical stripes.

Either direction works well, but if you want the same horizontal look of the pieced-stripe quilt, be sure the printed stripes run from selvage to selvage.

Fins with striped fabric, 48″ × 60″; designed, pieced, and quilted by Daisy Aschehoug; 2018

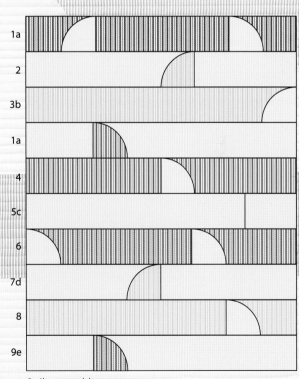

Quilt assembly

FESTOONS

FINISHED BLOCK: 7″ × 14″ • FINISHED QUILT: 70″ × 80½″

Festoons is loosely inspired by Edwardian decor and fashion, which often featured stripes softened by ruffles, puffs, and lace. Festoons uses improv stripes and bright colors to capture the feel of an outdoor festival.

MATERIALS

Yardages are based on 40″ usable width. (Fabrics in parentheses are by Robert Kaufman Fabrics.)

Fabric

CREAM STRIPE *(Kona Natural)*: ¾ yard

BLACK STRIPE *(Kona Black)*: ½ yard

KHAKI *(Kona Limestone)*: 4⅔ yards for background

DARK GRAY *(Kona Charcoal)*: ⅔ yard for arc units

YELLOW *(Kona Bright Idea)*: ⅔ yard for arc units

LIGHT AQUA *(Kona Sea Glass)*: ⅔ yard for arc units

PINK *(Kona Candy Pink)*: ⅔ yard for arc units

SAGE *(Kona Sage)*: ⅔ yard for arc units

LIGHT ORANGE *(Kona Papaya)*: ⅔ yard for arc units

PUNCH *(Kona Punch)*: ⅔ yard for arc units

ORANGE *(Kona Tangerine)*: ⅔ yard for arc units

BINDING: ¾ yard

BACKING: 5 yards

Other materials

BATTING: 78″ × 89″

TEMPLATES: Make templates from these patterns: 7″ Concave (page 123), 7″ Arc (page 127), and 3½″ Convex (page 124).

TIP

Make the Festoon blocks with solid Kona Natural or Kona Black centers and use a printed stripe or a print that reads as a stripe for the festoon colors.

If you'd like to use a printed stripe fabric instead of piecing the stripes, see Printed Stripe Option (page 65).

CUTTING

See Cutting Techniques (page 13) for more information about how to cut curves and use fabric efficiently.
See the cutting diagrams for concave and convex pieces (page 14).

FABRIC	CUT	SUBCUT		
		Rectangles, squares, and strips	7″ concave	7″ arc
Cream	5 strips 4½″ × WOF	Subcut freehand into pieces approximately 1½″–1¾″ wide × 4½″		
Black	3 strips 4½″ × WOF*	Subcut freehand into pieces approximately ¾″–1″ wide × 4½″.		
Khaki	11 strips 7½″ × WOF	2 strips 7½″ × 35½″ 2 strips 7½″ × 32″ 2 strips 7½″ × 28½″	48	
	10 strips 4″ × WOF	10 rectangles 4″ × 28½″		
	2 strips 18″ × WOF	2 rectangles 18″ × 35½″		
Color fabrics	**From *each* of the 8 fabrics:** 2 strips 7½″ × WOF (16 total)			6 arcs from each fabric (48 total)

* WOF = width of fabric

CONSTRUCTION

See Piecing Basics (page 15) for more details about how to sew, press, and trim the curves and stripes for this quilt.

Pieced Stripes

1. Improv sew the black and cream strips together alternating colors to make 4 or 5 strips 4½″ × at least 40″. Irregular or crooked seams are desirable when improv piecing.

TIP
Chain piece the black and cream strips for efficiency.

2. From the improv strips, subcut 48 convex pieces.

Festoons, 70″ × 84″; designed, pieced, and quilted by Heather Black; 2018

Festoon Block

TIP

Arrange all pieces by color and in the proper orientation before piecing, and sew the blocks in sets of matching pairs. This will help prevent piecing stripes in the wrong direction.

1. Make a double quarter-circle:

   Sew the convex piece to the arc first, then add the concave piece.

   • striped convex / color arc / khaki concave

2. Repeat with the pieces for a matching quarter-circle.

3. Sew the pair together to make a half-circle.

4. Repeat to make 24 blocks total.

Festoon block. Make 24 blocks.

Sashing and Borders

Sew the following khaki strips end to end:

• 2 strips 4″ × 28½″ to make a sashing strip 4″ × 56½″. Repeat to make 5 total.

• 1 strip 7½″ × 28½″ and 1 strip 7½″ × 32″ to make the right border strip 7½″ × 60″. Repeat for the left border.

• 2 strips 7½″ × 35½″ to make the top border strip 7½″ × 70½″.

• 2 strips 18″ × 35½″ to make the bottom border strip 18″ × 70½″.

Quilt Assembly

Refer to the quilt assembly diagram.

1. Sew the blocks into rows.

2. Sew the rows and sashing together.

3. Sew the right and left borders to the quilt body.

4. Sew the top and bottom borders to the quilt body to complete the top.

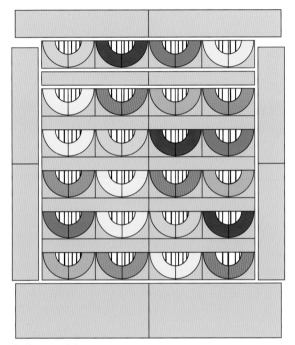

Quilt assembly

Finishing

Layer, quilt, and bind as desired.

PRINTED STRIPE OPTION

If you want to use a printed stripe, purchase
½ yard. Choose a print that mimics the feel of the
improv-pieced stripes. Cut 4 strips 4˝ × width of
fabric and subcut 48 convex pieces.

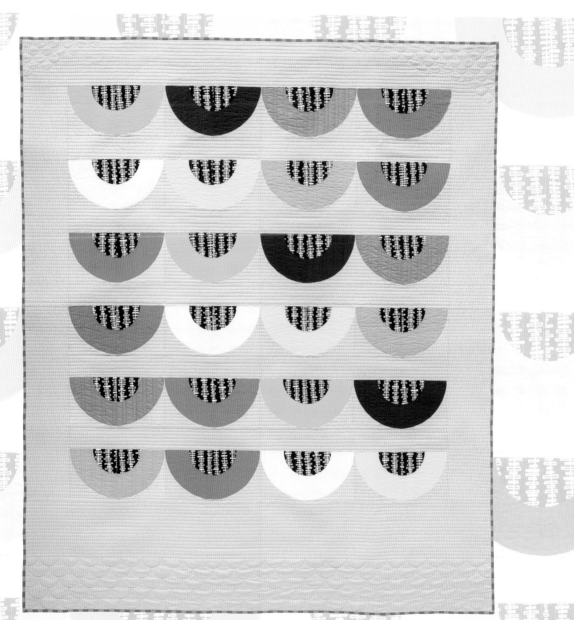

Festoons with printed stripes, 70˝ × 84˝; designed, pieced, and quilted by Heather Black; 2018

PORTALS

FINISHED BLOCK: 12″ × 12″ • FINISHED QUILT: 60″ × 73″

Portals is a fun sci-fi inspired design. Of the twenty portal blocks, only one is an open portal. What dangers or adventures lie on the other side? This design features a pieced stripe as a background to add movement and dimension.

MATERIALS

Yardages are based on 40″ usable width. (Fabrics in parentheses are by Robert Kaufman Fabrics.)

Fabric

GREEN (*Kona Cactus*): 2⅜ yards for background

GREEN 1 (*Kona Honey Dew*): 1 yard

GREEN 2 (*Kona Limelight*): 1 yard

GREEN 3 (*Kona Peapod*): 1 yard

DARK BLUE (*Kona Storm*): 2 yards

BLUE (*Kona Windsor*): 1 yard

LIGHT BLUE (*Kona Slate*): 1 yard

LIGHT ORANGE (*Kona Saffron*): 1 fat eighth

ORANGE (*Kona Kumquat*): 1 fat eighth

DARK ORANGE (*Kona Flame*): 1 fat eighth

RED (*Kona Paprika*): 1 fat eighth

LIGHT PURPLE (*Kona Petunia*): 1 fat eighth

AQUA (*Kona Aqua*): 1 fat eighth

BINDING: ⅝ yard

BACKING: 4½ yards

Other materials

BATTING: 68″ × 81″ (I used Warm & Natural by The Warm Company.)

TEMPLATES: Make templates from these patterns: 6″ Concave (page 124), 6″ Concave with 1″ Float (page 125), 3″ Convex (page 122), 6″ Convex (page 122), and 5″ Arc (page 126).

TIP

If you'd like to use a printed stripe fabric instead of piecing the stripes, see Printed Stripe Option (page 73).

CUTTING

See Cutting Techniques (page 13) for more information about how to cut curves and use fabric efficiently.
See the cutting diagrams for concave and convex pieces (page 14).

FABRIC	CUT	SUBCUT				
		Rectangles, squares, and strips	6″ convex	6″ concave with 1″ float	3″ convex	5″ arc
Green background	11 strips 1½″ × WOF*	8 rectangles 1½″ × 26″ 15 rectangles 1½″ × 12½″				
	4 strips 3½″ × WOF	2 rectangles 3½″ × 32½″ 2 rectangles 3½″ × 30½″				
	7 strips 6½″ × WOF	2 rectangles 6½″ × 32½″ 2 rectangles 6½″ × 30½″	19			
Light green, green, and dark green	**From *each* of the 3 fabrics:** 4 strips 6½″ × WOF (12 total)		19 (57 total)			
Dark blue	42 strips 1½″ × WOF					
Blue	21 strips 1½″ × WOF					
Light blue	21 strips 1½″ × WOF					
Light orange, orange, dark orange, and red				**From *each* of the 4 fabrics:** 1 (4 total)		
Light purple					4	
Aqua						4

* WOF = width of fabric

Portals, 60″ × 73″; designed, pieced, and quilted by Heather Black; 2018

CONSTRUCTION

See Piecing Basics (page 15) for more details about how to sew, press, and trim the curves and stripes for this quilt.

Closed Portal Block

Blue Stripe Concave Units

TIP

When sewing pieced stripes, change the direction of sewing to help keep the strip set from bowing.

STRIPED CONCAVE A

1. Using the 1½˝ strips and referring to the diagram for strip order, make a strip set:

   • 3 dark blue / 2 blue / 1 light blue

2. Repeat to make 7 total.

3. Subcut 38 concave pieces, using the 6˝ concave template.

Striped concave A

STRIPED CONCAVE B

1. Using the 1½˝ strips and referring to the diagram for strip order, make a strip set:

   • 3 dark blue / 1 blue / 2 light blue

2. Repeat to make 7 total.

3. Subcut 38 concave pieces, using the 6˝ concave template.

Striped concave B

Block Assembly

TIP

Arrange all pieces in the proper orientation before piecing, and work on 1 block at a time. This will help prevent piecing stripes in the wrong direction.

1. Make the following quarter-circles:

   • 1 striped concave A / light green convex

   • 1 striped concave A / green background convex

   • 1 striped concave B / dark green convex

   • 1 striped concave B / green convex unit.

2. Arrange the units to form a circle as shown. Sew the units in pairs, then join the pairs to complete the block.

3. Repeat to make 19 total.

Closed Portal block

TIP

Line up seams and pin at each color change.

Open Portal Block

1. Make the following double quarter-circles:

Sew the convex piece to the arc, then add the concave piece.

- light orange concave / aqua arc / light purple convex
- orange concave / aqua arc / light purple convex
- dark orange concave / aqua arc / light purple convex
- red concave / aqua arc / light purple convex

2. Arrange the units to form a circle as shown. Sew the units in pairs, then join the pairs to complete the block.

Open Portal block

Sashing and Borders

Sew the following green background strips end to end:

- 2 strips 1½″ × 26″
  to make a horizontal sashing strip 1½″ × 51½″.
  Repeat to make 4 total.
- 2 strips 3½″ × 32½″
  to make the left border strip 3½″ × 64½″
- 2 strip 3½″ × 30½″
  to make the top border strip 3½″ × 60½″
- 2 strips 6½″ × 32½″
  to make the right border strip 6½″ × 64½″
- 2 strips 6½″ × 30½″
  to make the bottom border strip 6½″ × 60½″

Quilt Assembly

Refer to the quilt assembly diagram.

1. Sew the blocks and 1½″ × 12½″ vertical sashing strips into rows.

2. Sew the rows together with the horizontal sashing strips.

3. Sew the right and left borders to the quilt body.

4. Sew the top and bottom borders to the quilt body to complete the quilt top.

Finishing

Layer, quilt, and bind as desired.

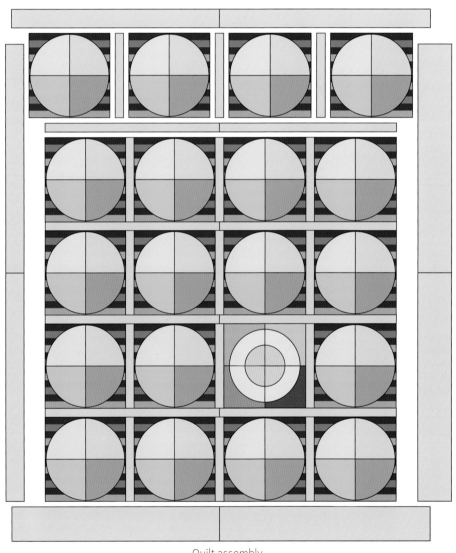

Quilt assembly

PRINTED STRIPE OPTION

If you want to use a printed stripe, purchase 1¾ yards of a tonal stripe print. (Yardage is based on a print where the stripe runs parallel to the selvage.) Cut 6 strips 6½″ × length of fabric; subcut 76 concave units using the 6″ concave template, making sure to cut them in matching sets of 4 (or 3 for fourth row), to keep rows correct.

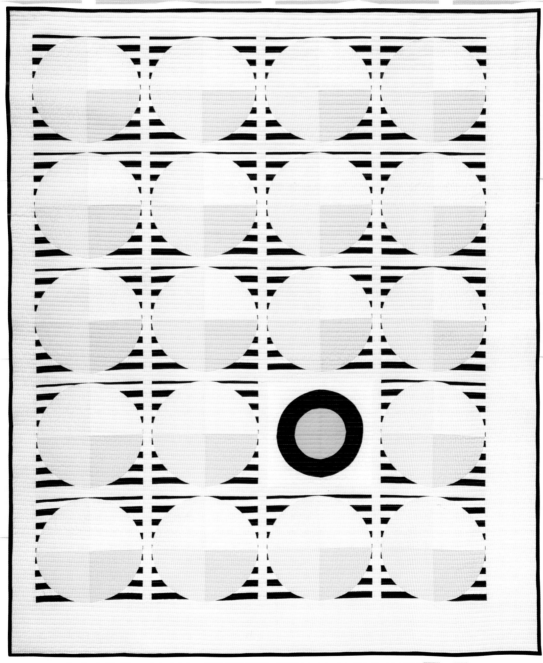

Portals with a printed stripe, 60″ × 72″; designed, pieced, and quilted by Heather Black; 2018

PREVAILING WINDS

FINISHED QUILT: 49″ × 56″

Prevailing Winds is a great crib-size or lap quilt. It was inspired by high- and
low-pressure systems illustrated on a weather map. This quilt is a great
way to use stripes and curves to create movement in a design.

MATERIALS

Yardages are based on 40″ usable width. (Fabrics in parentheses are by Robert Kaufman Fabrics.)

Fabric

LIGHT GRAY *(Kona Overcast)*: ⅝ yard

DARK GRAY *(Kona Graphite)*: ⅝ yard

LIGHT PURPLE *(Kona Petunia)*: ⅝ yard

DARK PURPLE *(Kona Lupine)*: ⅝ yard

AQUA *(Kona Spa Blue)*: 1⅓ yards

GOLD STRIPE *(Sevenberry Canvas Stripe Gold)*:
½ yard

NAVY STRIPE *(Sevenberry Canvas Stripe Navy)*:
½ yard

BINDING: ½ yard

BACKING: 3⅜ yards

Other materials

BATTING: 57″ × 64″ (I used Warm & Natural
by The Warm Company.)

TEMPLATES: Make templates from these patterns:
7″ Concave (page 123), 7″ Arc (page 127), and
3½″ Convex (page 124).

TIP

If you'd like to piece the stripes instead of using
a printed stripe fabric, see Pieced Stripe Option
(page 79).

CUTTING

See Cutting Techniques (page 13) for more information about how to cut curves and use fabric efficiently. See the cutting diagrams for concave and convex pieces (page 14).

Cutting diagram for stripe prints

FABRIC	CUT	SUBCUT			
		Rectangles, squares, and strips	7″ concave	3½″ convex	7″ arc
Light gray and light purple	**From *each* of the 2 fabrics, cut:** 1 strip 14½″ × WOF* (4 total)	1 square 14½″ × 14½″ (2 total) 1 rectangle 14½″ × 7½″ (2 total)	4 (8 total)		
Dark gray and dark purple	**From *each* of the 2 fabrics, cut:** 2 strips 7½″ × WOF (2 total)	1 strip 7½″ × 28½″ (2 total) 1 strip 7½″ × 21½″ (2 total)	2 (4 total)		
Aqua	4 strips 4″ × WOF	2 strips 4″ × 28½″ 2 strips 4″ × 35½″			
	3 strips 7½″ × WOF				12
Gold stripe and navy stripe	**From *each* of the 2 fabrics, cut:** 3 strips 4″ × WOF (4 total)	1 strip 4″ × 28½″ (2 total) 1 strip 4″ × 35½″ (2 total)		6* (12 total) See cutting diagram (above).	

* WOF = width of fabric

CONSTRUCTION

See Piecing Basics (page 15) for more details about how to sew, press, and trim the curves and stripes for this quilt.

Double Quarter-Circles

Sew the convex piece to the arc first, then add the concave piece.

TIP

Referring to the quilt assembly diagram (page 78), arrange each ¾ circle before piecing these units to ensure that convex stripe units are facing the correct direction.

1. Make the following double quarter-circles:

   • 1 dark gray concave / aqua arc / gold-striped convex

   • 2 light gray concave / aqua arc / gold-striped convex

Prevailing Winds, 49″ × 56″; designed, pieced, and quilted by Heather Black; 2018

2. Repeat to make another set of 3.

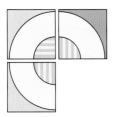

3. Make the following double quarter-circles:

- 1 dark purple concave / aqua arc / navy-striped convex

- 2 light purple concave / aqua arc / navy-striped convex

4. Repeat to make another set of 3.

Quilt Assembly

Refer to the quilt assembly diagram (at right).

Row 1

1. Sew the quarter-circles with the light gray concave pieces together as shown. Sew the 7½″ × 14½″ light gray rectangle to the left side of the unit.

2. Sew the quarter-circle with the dark gray concave piece to the dark gray 7½″ × 28½″ rectangle.

3. Sew a gold stripe 4″ × 35½″ strip to an aqua 4″ × 35½″ strip.

4. Sew the unit from Step 2 to the top of the unit from Step 3.

5. Sew the unit from Step 1 to the unit from Step 4 to complete the row.

Row 3

Repeat Row 1, Steps 1–4, except use a 14½″ × 14½″ square in Step 1.

Rows 2 and 4

Follow the same process as Rows 1 and 3, referring to the quilt assembly diagram for sizes of the setting pieces and their reversed placement.

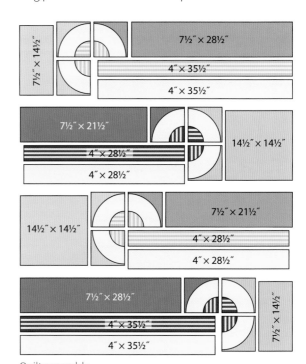

Quilt assembly

Finishing

Layer, quilt, and bind as desired.

PIECED STRIPES OPTION

If you choose to piece stripes, purchase ½ yard each of orange, yellow, and cream fabric. Cut the following strips 1″ × width of fabric: 12 orange, 12 yellow, and 18 cream. Make 3 yellow/cream strip sets, each with 4 yellow and 3 cream strips, alternating colors. Repeat the process for orange and cream 1″ strips.

 TIP

When sewing strips into strip sets, change the direction of sewing with each strip to help keep the strip set from bowing.

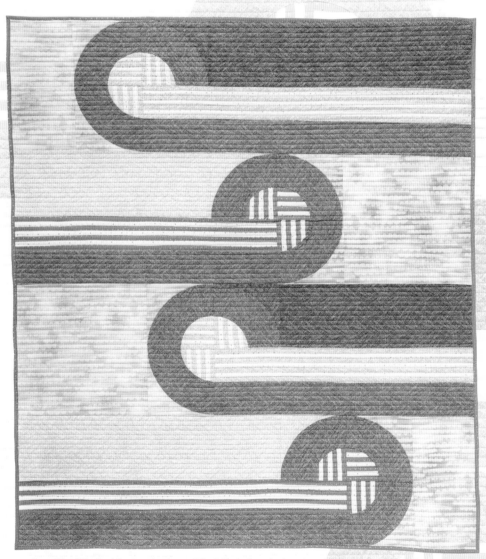

Prevailing Winds with pieced stripes, 49″ × 56″; designed, pieced, and quilted by Heather Black; 2018

Fabric: Lou Lou by Emmie K for Robert Kaufman Fabrics

CONCERT

FINISHED QUILT: 48″ × 63″

Concert creates a visual symphony of stripes, curves, and the colors from a favorite color palette. The repetition of smaller pieces makes this design perfect for using treasured scraps that are at least 1½″ × 7″.

MATERIALS

Yardages are based on 40″ usable width. (Fabrics in parentheses are by Robert Kaufman Fabrics.)

Fabric

BLUE *(Kona Slate)*: 3¼ yards

DARK BLUE *(Kona Windsor)*:

⅔ yard for piecing

½ yard for binding

PINK *(Kona Rose)*: ⅓ yard

LIGHT PINK *(Kona Dusty Peach)*: ⅛ yard

BLACK *(Kona Black)*: ⅛ yard

CHARCOAL *(Kona Charcoal)*: ⅛ yard

TEAL *(Kona Teal Blue)*: ⅛ yard

LIGHT TEAL *(Kona Sage)*: ⅛ yard

LIGHT BLUE *(Kona Ice Frappe)*: ⅛ yard

PALE PINK *(Kona Shell)*: 5¼ yards for background

BACKING: 3⅛ yards

Other materials

BATTING: 56″ × 71″

TEMPLATES: Make templates from these patterns: 6″ Concave (page 124) and 6″ Convex (page 122).

TIP

If you'd like to use a printed stripe fabric instead of piecing the stripes, see Printed Stripe Option (page 85).

CUTTING

See Cutting Techniques (page 13) for more information about how to cut curves and use fabric efficiently. See the cutting diagram for concave pieces (page 14).

FABRIC	CUT	SUBCUT	
		Rectangles, squares, and strips	6″ concave
Blue	57 strips 1½″ × WOF*	**From *each* strip, subcut:** 2 rectangles 1½″ × 16½″ (100 total)	
Dark blue	11 strips 1½″ × WOF	**From *each* strip, subcut:** 2 rectangles 1½″ × 16½″ (22 total)	
Pink	5 strips 1½″ × WOF	**From *each* strip, subcut:** 2 rectangles 1½″ × 16½″ (10 total)	
Light pink, black, charcoal, teal, light teal, light blue	**From *each* of the 6 colors:** 2 strips 1½″ × WOF (12 total)	**From *each* strip, subcut:** 2 rectangles 1½″ × 16½″ (24 total)	
Pale pink	7 strips 6½″ × WOF		64
	2 strips 6½″ × WOF		
	1 strip 6½″ × WOF	2 rectangles 6½″ × 8½″	
	1 strip 3½″ × WOF		
	1 strip 3½″ × WOF	1 rectangle 3½″ × 8½″	
	72 strips 1½″ × WOF	143 rectangles 1½″ × 16½″	

* WOF = width of fabric

Concert, 48″ × 63″; designed, pieced, and quilted by Daisy Aschehoug; 2018

CONSTRUCTION

See Piecing Basics (page 15) for more details about how to sew, press, and trim the curves and stripes for this quilt.

Striped Quarter-Circles

Striped Convex Units

1. Using the 1½″ × 16½″ rectangles, make a strip set by alternating 14 assorted color rectangles and 13 pale pink rectangles. Press the seams open.

2. Repeat to make 11 total.

3. From each strip set, subcut 6 convex pieces until you have 64. Align the template so that the seam runs along the center of the template, with 32 of the convex pieces having a pale pink stripe along the left of center and the other 32 convex pieces with the pale pink stripe to the right of center.

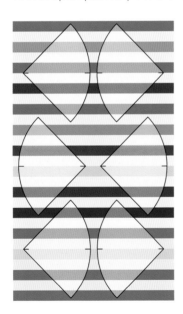

Quarter-Circle Assembly

1. Make a quarter-circle:

   • pale pink concave / striped convex

2. Repeat to make 64 total.

Sashing and Borders

Sew the following pale pink strips end to end:

   • 1 rectangle 3½″ × 8½″ and 1 strip 3½″ × width of fabric.
   Trim to 3½″ × 48½″ for the horizontal sashing.

   • 1 rectangle 6½″ × 8½″ and 1 strip 6½″ × width of fabric.
   Trim to 6½″ × 48½″ for the top border. Repeat for the bottom border.

Quilt Construction

Refer to the quilt assembly diagram.

1. Sew the blocks into rows.

2. Sew the rows together, with the horizontal sashing strip in the center.

3. Add the top and bottom borders to complete the quilt top.

Finishing

Layer, quilt, and bind as desired.

Quilt assembly

PRINTED STRIPE OPTION

This quilt uses small yardages of 11 different prints for the stripes. But you could substitute ⅝ yard of 4 different striped prints or 2¼ yards of a single striped print. The design requires 16 strips 6½″ × the width of fabric and 2¼ yards of background fabric. From each of the 16 strips, cut 4 convex pieces (64 total).

Concert with printed stripes, 48″ × 63″; designed, pieced, and quilted by Daisy Aschehoug; 2018

ROUCHED

FINISHED QUILT: 27″ × 45″

Rouched uses a monochromatic palette and long, skinny strips radiating off a center formation of curves. Create a wallhanging to complement your decor or pick a few different shades of a small child's favorite color for a carseat or stroller quilt.

MATERIALS

Yardages are based on 40″ usable width. (Fabrics in parentheses are by Robert Kaufman Fabrics.)

Fabric

PINK *(Kona Rose)*: 1½ yards

LIGHT PINK *(Kona Dusty Peach)*: ½ yard

PALE PINK *(Kona Pearl Pink)*: ⅔ yard

DARK PINK *(Kona Deep Rose)*:

   1⅔ yards for piecing

   ½ yard for binding

BACKING: 1½ yards

Other materials

BATTING: 35″ × 53″

TEMPLATES: Make templates from these patterns: 6″ Concave (page 124) and 6″ Convex (page 122).

CUTTING

See Cutting Techniques (page 13) for more information about how to cut curves and use fabric efficiently. See the cutting diagrams for concave pieces (page 14).

FABRIC	CUT	SUBCUT
		6″ concave ⌐
Pink	45 strips 1″ × WOF*	
Light pink	12 strips 1″ × WOF	
Pale pink	15 strips 1″ × WOF	
Dark pink	36 strips 1″ × WOF	
	1 strip 6½″ × WOF	10

* WOF = width of fabric

CONSTRUCTION

Instead of making quarter-circle units as in the other projects, in this quilt you will make striped rectangles, use the convex template to trim one end to a quarter-circle shape, then add the concave piece to replace the rectangle corner. It looks complicated, but it's not any harder than the usual quarter-circles.

See Piecing Basics (page 15) for more details about how to sew, press, and trim the curves and stripes for this quilt.

Dark Pink / Pink Striped Rectangles

1. Make a strip set with 6 dark pink and 6 pink 1 × WOF strips, alternating colors. Press the seams open.

2. Repeat to make 6 total.

3. Subcut the following:

   • 6 rectangles 6½″ × 20½″ (Set 1 aside.)

   • 1 rectangle 6½″ × 15½″ (Set aside.)

   • 1 rectangle 6½″ × 12½″

4. Align the convex template on the right end of 2 striped 20½″ rectangles and the 12½″ rectangle. Trim along the curved edge.

5. Repeat the process on the left end of 3 of the 20½″ striped rectangles.

6. Sew a dark pink concave piece to the curved end of each rectangle from Steps 4 and 5, 6 total.

Assorted Pink Striped Rectangles

1. Make a strip set with 3 pink, 5 pale pink, and 4 light pink strips, randomly placing colors. Press the seams open.

2. Repeat to make 3 total.

3. Subcut the following:

   • 3 rectangles 6½″ × 20½″

   • 2 rectangles 6½″ × 10½″ (Set 1 aside.)

4. Align the convex template on the right end of 2 of the 20½″ rectangles. Trim along the curved edge.

5. Repeat the process on the left end of a 20½″ rectangle and a 10½″ rectangle.

6. Sew a dark pink concave piece to the curved end of each rectangle from Steps 4 and 5, 4 total.

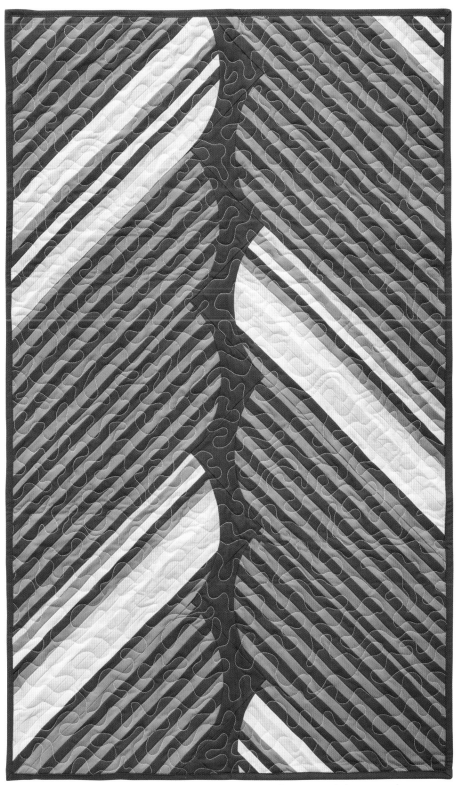

Rouched, 27″ × 45″; designed, pieced, and quilted by Daisy Aschehoug; 2018

Quilt Assembly

Refer to the quilt assembly diagram (next page).

1. Arrange the units as shown. Starting at the bottom of the quilt, sew the lower right rectangle to the bottom edge of the left rectangle above it.

2. Sew the pieced edge of the unit from Step 1 to the bottom edge of the rectangle now at the bottom right.

3. Sew the unit from Step 2 to the bottom edge of the rectangle at the bottom left.

4. Continue the pattern, adding a right rectangle and then a left rectangle to resemble a braid. Match the top left rectangle to the seam of the pieced unit. Center the top right 10½″ rectangle on top of the 20½″ rectangle.

5. When you have assembled the top, trim the sides first by lining up your rotary ruler with the bottom 3 inside points on each side. Then trim the top and bottom to be square with the sides. It will be approximately 27½″ × 45½″.

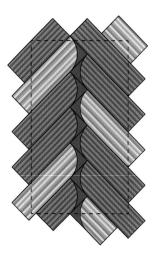

Finishing

Layer, quilt, and bind as desired.

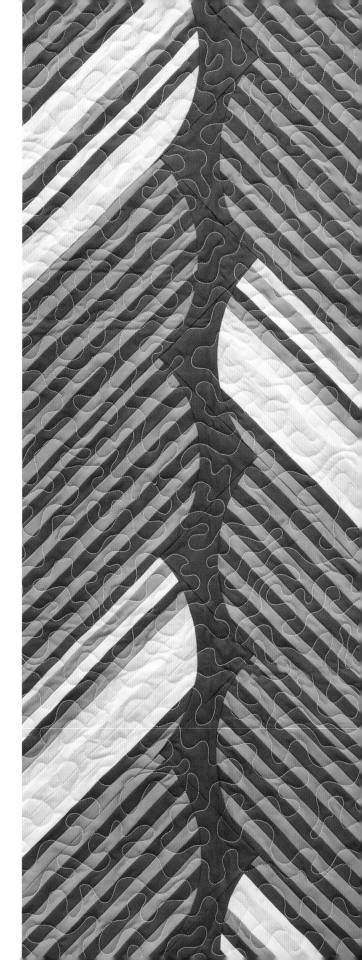

Quilt assembly

SUNSET HORIZONS

FINISHED BLOCK: 14″ × 14″ • FINISHED QUILT: 56″ × 66½″

Just like looking at the sun melt into an ocean, *Sunset Horizons* captures the
moment the sun "touches" the sea. By piecing a circle within a circle, this
quilt creates the illusion of looking through a window at the sunset.

MATERIALS

Yardages are based on 40″ usable width. (Fabrics in parentheses are by Robert Kaufman Fabrics.)

Fabric

CREAM *(Essex Linen Linen)*: 4⅓ yards background

DARK PINK *(Essex Linen Rose)*: ⅜ yard

PINK *(Essex Linen Peach)*: ¼ yard

DARK BLUE *(Essex Linen Slate)*: ⅜ yard

BLUE *(Essex Linen Dusty Blue)*: ¼ yard

DARK TAN *(Essex Linen Leather)*: ⅜ yard

TAN *(Essex Linen Sand)*: ¼ yard

DARK GRAY *(Essex Linen Graphite)*: ⅜ yard

GRAY *(Essex Linen Smoke)*: ¼ yard

BINDING: ⅔ yard

BACKING: 3⅝ yards

Other materials

BATTING: 64″ × 75″ (I used Warm & Natural
by The Warm Company.)

TEMPLATES: Make templates from these patterns:
3″ Convex (page 122), 6″ Convex (page 124),
3″ Cutaway (page 123), and 6″ Cutaway (page 123).

TIP

If you'd like to use a printed stripe fabric instead
of piecing the stripes, see Printed Stripe Option
(page 99).

CUTTING

See Cutting Techniques (page 13) for more information about how to cut curves and use fabric efficiently.
See the cutting diagrams for concave and convex pieces (page 14).

FABRIC	CUT	SUBCUT			
		Rectangles, squares, and strips	Concave squares using 6″ cutaway	3″ convex	Concave rectangles using 3″ cutaway
Cream	16 strips 7½″ × WOF*	6 strips 7½″ × 28½″	48, from 7½″ × 7½″ squares. See squares cutting diagram (below).		
	2 strips 4″ × WOF	2 strips 4″ × 28½″			
	4 strips 3½″ × WOF			48	
	4 strips 1″ × WOF				
Dark pink, dark blue, dark tan, and dark gray	From *each* of the 4 colors: 2 strips 3½″ × WOF (8 total)				12 (48 total), from 3½″ × 6½″ rectangles. See rectangles cutting diagram (below) for which corners to cut away.
	1 strip 1½″ × WOF (4 total)				
	1 strip 1″ × WOF (4 total)				
Pink, blue, tan, and gray	From *each* of the 4 fabrics: 1 strip 1½″ × WOF (4 total)				
	2 strips 2″ × WOF (8 total)				

* WOF = width of fabric

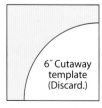

Concave squares cutting diagram. Make 3 sets in each fabric.

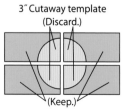

Concave rectangles cutting diagram

Sunset Horizons, 56″ × 66½″; designed, pieced, and quilted by Heather Black; 2018

CONSTRUCTION

See Piecing Basics (page 15) for more details about how to sew, press, and trim the curves and stripes for this quilt.

Sunset Horizon Blocks

Sun Half-Block

 TIP

Arrange each block in the proper orientation before piecing, and work on 1 block at a time. This will help prevent piecing stripes and/or curves in the wrong direction.

1. Arrange a set of dark pink concave rectangles as shown. Sew a 3″ cream convex piece to each rectangle.

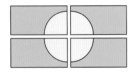

2. Sew the left 2 rectangles together and the right 2 rectangles together.

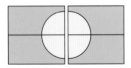

3. Use the 6″ convex template to trim the units from Step 2 into convex pieces. See the diagram for how to place the template.

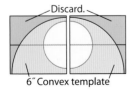

Discard.

6″ Convex template

4. Sew a convex piece from Step 3 to a cream concave piece, creating 1 sun quarter-circle piece. Repeat with the other convex pieces.

5. Sew the units from Step 4 together to complete the upper half-block.

6. Repeat Steps 1–5 to make 2 more pink half-blocks, 3 blue, 3 tan, and 3 gray.

Horizon Half-Block

1. Make a strip set using width-of-fabric strips in the following order:

- 1½″ pink strip
- 1½″ dark pink strip
- 1″ cream strip
- 2″ pink strip
- 1″ dark pink strip
- 2″ pink strip

1½″
1″
2″
1″
2″

2. Subcut 6 striped squares 6½″ × 6½″. Set 4 aside.

From 2 striped squares, cut a convex piece using the 6″ convex template. See the cutting diagram to see how to place the template.

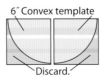

6″ Convex template

Discard.

3. Make a quarter-circle with an off-white concave and striped convex piece. Repeat with the remaining striped convex piece.

4. Sew the quarter-circle units together to complete the lower half-block.

5. Repeat Steps 1–4 to make 2 more pink half-blocks, 3 blue, 3 tan, and 3 gray.

Block Assembly

1. Sew the sun half-block to the horizon half-block as shown to complete the block.

2. Repeat to make 3 blocks in each color—pink, blue, tan, and gray.

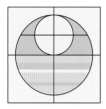

Sashing and Borders

Sew the following strips end to end:

- 2 strips 4″ × 28½″
  to make the top border 4″ × 56½″

- 2 strips 7½″ × 28½″
  to make the bottom border 7½″ × 56½″.

Repeat for the left and right borders.

Quilt Assembly

Refer to the quilt assembly diagram.

1. Sew the blocks into rows.

2. Sew the rows together.

3. Sew the right and left borders to the quilt body.

4. Sew the top and bottom borders to the quilt body to complete the top.

Finishing

Layer, quilt, and bind as desired.

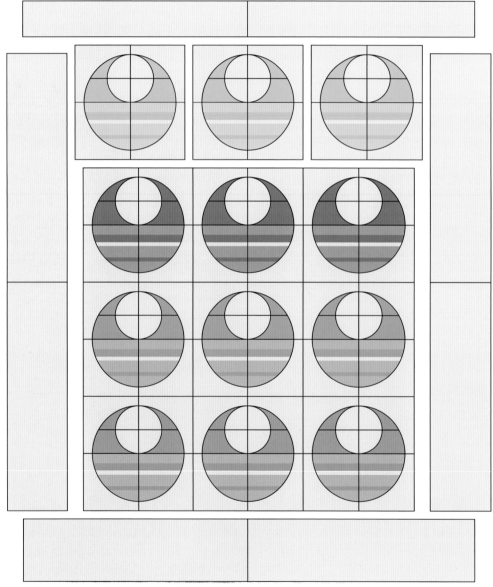

Quilt assembly

PRINTED STRIPE OPTION

For a printed stripe, purchase 1 yard of tonal striped fabric. Cut 24 convex pieces using the 6˝ convex template.

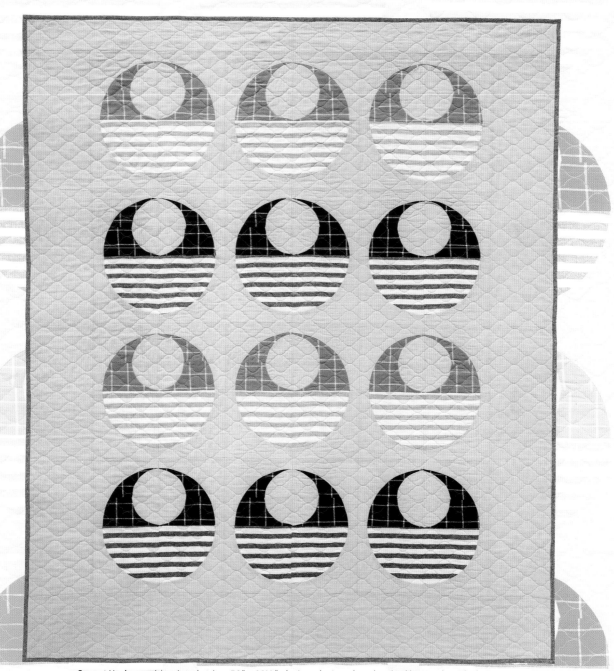

Sunset Horizons with printed stripe, 56˝ × 66½˝; designed, pieced, and quilted by Heather Black; 2018

TIDBITS

FINISHED BLOCK: 12″ × 12″ • FINISHED QUILT: 60″ × 72″

Tidbits is a great design for jumping into using stripes with curves since there are no stripes that line up. As the name suggests, the *tidbit*—often used to describe an interesting piece of information or gossip—is in each block. The shape of the blocks looks similar to conversation bubbles, and the swirling stripe within keeps the quilt interesting, just like a juicy tidbit.

MATERIALS

Yardages are based on 40″ usable width. (Fabrics in parentheses are by Robert Kaufman Fabrics.)

Fabric

BLUE *(Manchester Blue)*: 1⅓ yards

PURPLE *(Manchester Violet)*: 1⅓ yards

LIGHT GRAY *(Manchester Shadow)*: 1⅛ yards

DARK GRAY *(Manchester Charcoal)*: 1⅛ yards

CREAM *(Manchester Ivory)*: 3 yards

BINDING: ¾ yard

BACKING: 3⅞ yards

Other materials

BATTING: 68″ × 80″ (I used Warm & Natural by The Warm Company.)

TEMPLATES: Make templates from these patterns: 6″ Concave (page 124), 6″ Arc (page 126), and 4″ Convex (page 122).

TIPS: FABRICS

- If you'd like to use a printed stripe fabric instead of piecing the stripes, see Printed Stripe Option (page 105).

- The Manchester fabrics are a looser weave that traditional quilting cottons. When using a lighter fabric, press with starch or a nonstarch alternative, such as Flatter (by Soak), to prevent warping of lines in strip sets.

CUTTING

See Cutting Techniques (page 13) for more information about how to cut curves and use fabric efficiently. See the cutting diagram for the concave pieces (page 14).

FABRIC	CUT	SUBCUT		
		Rectangles, squares, and strips	6″ concave	6″ arc
Blue and purple	**From *each* of the 2 colors:** 40 strips 1″ × WOF* (80 total)			
Light gray and dark gray	**From *each* of the 2 colors:** 4 strips 6½″ × WOF (8 total)			30 (60 total)
	3 strips 2½″ × WOF (6 total)	10 rectangles 2½″ × 4½″ (20 total) 10 rectangles 2½″ × 6½″ (20 total)		
Cream	6 strips 6½″ × WOF		60	
	4 strips 9½″ × WOF	4 strips 9½″ × 30½″		
	4 strips 3½″ × WOF	4 strips 3½″ × 30½″		

* WOF = width of fabric

CONSTRUCTION

See Piecing Basics (page 15) for more details about how to sew, press, and trim the curves and stripes for this quilt.

Tidbit Blocks

Striped Convex Units

TIP

When sewing pieced stripes, always keep the same color on the top. This will automatically change the direction of sewing and help keep the strip set from bowing.

1. Using the 1″ strips, sew 4 blue strips and 4 purple strips together, alternating colors. Repeat for a total of 10 strip sets.

2. Subcut:

- 20 squares 4½″ × 4½″

- 60 convex pieces using the 4″ convex template. See the cutting diagram (below).

TIP

When cutting convex units keep the template facing the same direction.

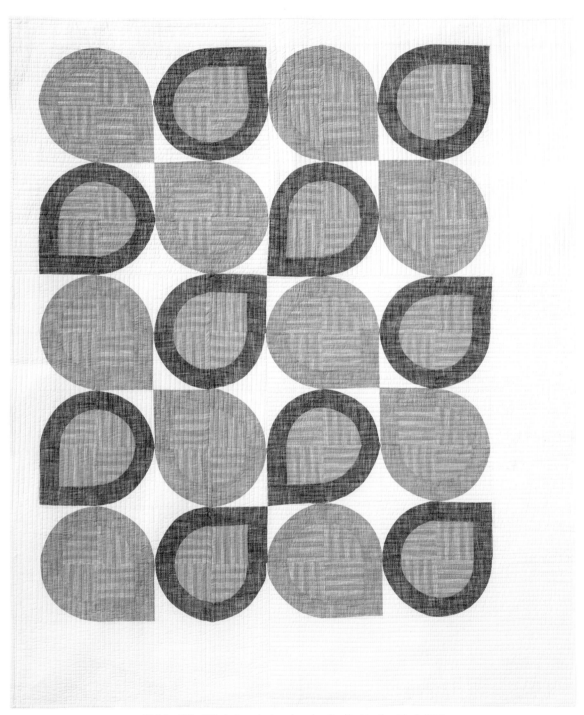

Tidbits, 60˝ × 72˝; designed, pieced, and quilted by Heather Black; 2018

Block Assembly

TIP
Arrange all the pieces in a block formation before piecing. This will help prevent piecing the stripes in the wrong direction.

1. Make a double quarter-circle:

- striped convex / gray arc / cream concave

Sew the convex piece to the arc first, then add the concave piece.

2. Repeat to make 3 total.

3. Sew a gray 2½″ × 4½″ rectangle to the bottom of a blue/purple 4½″ square.

4. Sew a gray strip 2½″ × 6½″ to the right of the unit from Step 3.

5. Arrange the 3 quarter-circles and the pieced square as shown. Sew the units together in pairs, then join the pairs to complete the block.

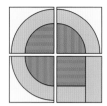
Tidbit block

6. Repeat Steps 1–5 to make 10 blocks with gray arcs and 10 blocks with dark gray arcs.

Sashing and Borders

Sew the following end to end:

- 2 strips 3½″ × 30½″ to make a top border strip 3½″ × 60½″. Repeat for the left border.

- 2 strips 9½″ × 30½″ to make a bottom border strip 9½″ × 60½″. Repeat for the right border.

Quilt Assembly

1. Sew the blocks into rows.

2. Sew the rows together.

3. Sew the right and left borders to the quilt body.

4. Sew the top and bottom borders to the quilt body to complete the top.

Finishing

Layer, quilt, and bind as desired.

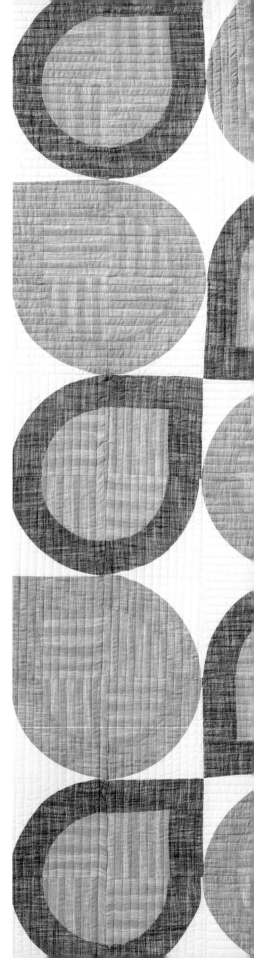

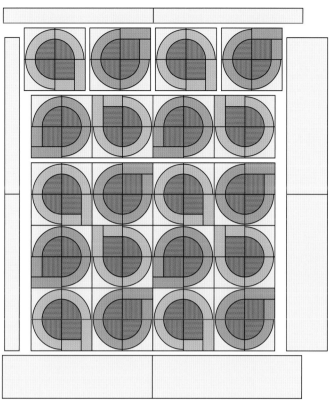

Quilt assembly

PRINTED STRIPE OPTION

If you want to use a printed stripe, purchase 1½ yards. Cut 10 strips 4½˝ × width of fabric. Subcut 60 convex units with the 4½˝ convex template and 20 squares 4½˝ × 4½˝.

Tidbits with a printed stripe, 60˝ × 72˝; designed, pieced, and quilted by Heather Black; 2018

AURORA

FINISHED BLOCK: 14″ × 14″ • FINISHED QUILT: 60″ × 72″

Aurora mixes the horizons of three stages of the day—morning, noon, and night. Horizontal stripes are very calming and make a great backdrop to set off any type of curve piecing.

MATERIALS

Yardages are based on 40″ usable width. (Fabrics in parentheses are by Robert Kaufman Fabrics.)

Fabric

TEAL *(Kona Teal Blue)*: ¼ yard

BLUE *(Kona Waterfall)*: ¾ yard

CREAM *(Kona Bone)*: 1½ yards

YELLOW *(Kona Curry)*: ⅔ yard

DARK PINK *(Kona Rose)*: ⅔ yard

PINK *(Kona Bellini)*: 1¼ yards

ORANGE *(Kona Tangerine)*: ¼ yard

OFF-WHITE *(Kona Haze)*: 2⅓ yards

BINDING: ¾ yard (or just ½ yard, if you choose to piece the center of the sides)

BACKING: 3¾ yards

Other materials

BATTING: 68″ × 80″ (I used Warm & Natural by The Warm Company.)

TEMPLATES: Make templates from these patterns: 7″ Concave (page 123), 3½″ Convex (page 124), and 7″ Arc (page 127).

TIP

If you'd like to use a printed stripe fabric instead of piecing the stripes, see Printed Stripe Option (page 113).

CUTTING

See Cutting Techniques (page 13) for more information about how to cut curves and use fabric efficiently. See the cutting diagram for convex pieces (page 14).

FABRIC	CUT	SUBCUT		
		Rectangles, squares, and strips	3½″ convex ⬭	7″ arc ⌒
Teal	4 strips 1½″ × WOF*	2 strips 1½″ × 32½″ 2 rectangles 1½″ × 14½″ (or 1½″ × 20″ **) 4 rectangles 1½″ × 7½″		
Blue	1 strip 4″ × WOF		4	
	7 strips 2½″ × WOF	4 strips 2½″ × 32½″ 4 rectangles 2½″ × 14½″ (or 2½″ × 20″ **) 8 rectangles 2½″ × 7½″		
Cream	3 strips 7½″ × WOF			12
	6 strips 1½″ × WOF	Subcut from *each*: 1 strip 1½″ × 32½″ (6 total) 1 rectangle 1½″ × 7½″ (6 total)		
	3 strips 1½″ × WOF (or 4 strips **)	6 rectangles 1½″ × 14½″ (6 total) (or 1½″ × 20″ **) 3 rectangles 1½″ × 7½″ (3 total)		
	1 strips 1½″ × WOF	3 rectangles 1½″ × 7½″		
Yellow	1 strip 4″ × WOF		4	
	7 strips 1½″ × WOF (or 8 strips **)	4 strips 1½″ × 32½″ 4 rectangles 1½″ × 14½″ (or 1½″ × 20″ **) 8 rectangles 1½″ × 7½″		
Dark pink	3 strips 4½″ × WOF	2 strips 4½″ × 32½″ 2 rectangles 4½″ × 14½″ (or 4½″ × 20″ **)		
	2 strips 2½″ × WOF	8 rectangles 2½″ × 7½″		
Pink	2 strips 6½″ × WOF	1 strip 6½″ × 32½″ 1 rectangle 6½″ × 14½″ (or 6½″ × 20″ **)		
	1 strip 4″ × WOF		4	
	3 strips 3½″ × WOF	2 strips 3½″ × 32½″ 2 rectangles 3½″ × 14½″ 4 rectangles 3½″ × 7½″		
	1 strip 2½″ × WOF	4 rectangles 2½″ × 7½″		
	1 strip 1½″ × WOF	4 rectangles 1½″ × 7½″		

FABRIC	CUT	SUBCUT		
		Rectangles, squares, and strips	3½″ convex ◿	7″ arc ◜
Orange	4 strips 1½″ × WOF	2 strips 1½″ × 32½″ 2 rectangles 1½″ × 14½″ (or 1½″ × 20″ **) 4 rectangles 1½″ × 7½″		
Off-white	2 strips 10½″ × WOF	1 strip 10½″ × 28½″ 1 strip 10½″ × 32½″		
	2 strips 20½″ × WOF	1 strip 20½″ × 28½″ 1 strip 20½″ × 32½″		

*WOF = width of fabric   ** Only if adding a pieced binding*

Aurora, 60″ × 72″; designed, pieced, and quilted by Heather Black; 2018

CONSTRUCTION

See Piecing Basics (page 15) for more details about how to sew, press, and trim the curves and stripes for this quilt.

Pieced Stripes

TIP

When sewing pieced stripes change the direction of sewing to help keep the strip set from bowing.

Strip Sets A and C

1. Referring to the diagram for strip order, make a strip set with the following:

   • 1 teal strip 1½″ × 32½″

   • 2 blue strips 2½″ × 32½″

   • 2 cream strips 1½″ × 32½″

   • 2 yellow strips 1½″ × 32½″

   • 1 pink strip 3½″ × 32½″

2. Repeat to make 2 strip sets total.

3. Using the same strip colors and order as Step 1, make a short strip set with the 14½″ rectangles (or 20″ rectangles *only if adding a pieced binding*).

4. Repeat to make 2 short strip sets total.

5. *Only if adding a pieced binding:* From each strip set, cut 1 rectangle 14½″ and 2 binding pieces 2½″.

Strip Set B

1. Referring to the diagram for strip order, make a strip set with the following:

   • 2 dark pink strips 4½″ × 32½″

   • 2 orange strips 1½″ × 32½″

   • 2 cream strips 1½″ × 32½″

   • 1 pink strip 6½″ × 32½″

2. Using the same strip colors and order as Step 1, make a short strip set with the 14½″ rectangles (or 20″ rectangles *only if adding a pieced binding*).

3. *Only if adding a pieced binding:* Subcut 1 strip set to 14½″ and 2 binding pieces 2½″.

Sun Block

TIP

Arrange all blocks in the proper orientation before piecing. This will help prevent piecing stripes in the wrong direction.

Stripe Concave Units

BLOCKS A AND C

1. Make a 7½″ square in the following order:

   • 1 teal strip 1½″ × 7½″

   • 1 blue strip 2½″ × 7½″

   • 1 cream strip 1½″ × 7½″

   • 1 yellow strip 1½″ × 7½″

   • 1 pink strip 2½″ × 7½″

2. Repeat to make 4 total.

3. Make a 7½″ square in the following order:

   • 1 pink strip 1½″ × 7½″

   • 1 yellow strip 1½″ × 7½″

   • 1 blue strip 2½″ × 7½″

   • 1 cream strip 1½″ × 7½″

   • 1 dark pink strip 2½″ × 7½″

4. Repeat to make 4 total.

5. Referring to the diagram (below Step 6), arrange 2 squares from Step 2 and 2 squares from Step 4 to match Strip Sets A and C (previous page).

6. Cut a concave piece from each square, using the 7″ concave template. See the diagram for how to place the template.

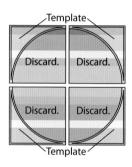

7. Repeat Steps 5 and 6 with the matching remaining squares from Steps 2 and 4.

BLOCK B

1. Make a 7½″ square in the following order:

- 1 dark pink strip 2½″ × 7½″

- 1 orange strip 1½″ × 7½″

- 1 cream strip 1½″ × 7½″

- 1 pink strip 3½″ × 7½″

2. Repeat to make 4 total.

3. Arrange 4 squares from Step 2 to match Strip Set B (previous page), with dark pink at the top and bottom of the four-patch arrangement.

4. Cut a concave piece from each square, using the 7″ concave template. See the Block B diagram (below right) for how to place the template.

Sun Block Assembly

BLOCKS A AND C

1. Make the following double quarter-circles, referring to the diagram for stripe placement:

- 2 striped concave from Blocks A and C Step 2 / cream arc / yellow convex

- 2 striped concave from Blocks A and C Step 4 / cream arc / yellow convex

2. Sew the units in pairs, then sew the pairs together to complete the block.

3. Repeat to make a second block with blue convex pieces for Block C.

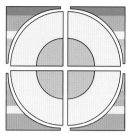

Block A

4. Make the following double quarter-circles, referring to the diagram for stripe placement:

- 4 striped concave from Block B / cream arc / pink convex

5. Sew the units in pairs, then sew the pairs together to complete the block.

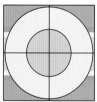

Block B

Sashing and Borders

Sew the following strips end to end:

- 1 off-white strip 10½″ × 28½″ and 1 off-white strip 10½″ × 32½″ to make the top border 10½″ × 60½″.

- 1 off-white strip 20½″ × 28½″ to 1 off-white strip 20½″ × 32½″ to make the bottom border 20½″ × 60½″.

Quilt Assembly

Refer to the quilt assembly diagram.

TIP

Line up seams and place a pin at each color change.

1. Sew 14½″ strip sets, Sun blocks, and 32½″ strip sets together in columns.

2. Sew the columns together

3. Sew the top and bottom borders to the quilt body to complete the top.

Finishing

Layer, quilt, and bind as desired.

Only if adding a pieced binding: Sew 2½″ Strip Sets A, B, and C in order to match the quilt sides. Add the solid binding to continue the sides and for the top and bottom.

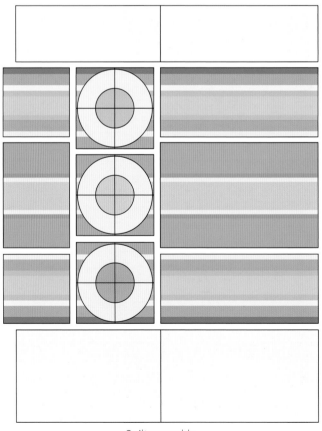

Quilt assembly

PRINTED STRIPE OPTION

If you want to use a printed stripe, purchase 3 yards of a multistripe print. (Yardage is based on a print where the stripe runs perpendicular to the selvage. The print repeat can mimic stripes without a true line.)

- Cut 3 strips 21½″ × width of fabric; subcut 2 strips 21½″ × 32½″ and 2 strips 21½″ × 14½″.

- Fussy cut 12 squares 7½″ × 7½″, matching the strips on the previously cut strips; subcut 12 squares with the 7″ concave template.

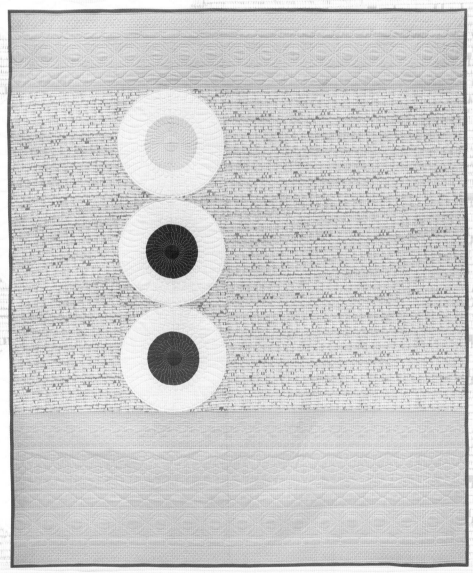

Aurora with printed stripes, 60″ × 72″; designed, pieced, and quilted by Heather Black; 2018

PATIO LIGHTS

FINISHED QUILT: 45″ × 60″

There's nothing more inviting than twinkling patio lights crisscrossed over a big outdoor dining table or a small corner of a garden. Whether you use alternating stripes or an improvised mix of colors, the contrasting curves that break the lines in this design add warmth and softness.

MATERIALS

Yardages are based on 40″ usable width. (Fabrics in parentheses are by Robert Kaufman Fabrics.)

Fabric

PINK *(Kona Shell)*: 1¾ yards

YELLOW *(Kona Canary)*: ⅝ yard

BLUES *(Kona Waterfall)*: 60 precut 2½″ strips (2 packs of Roll Ups; you'll have leftovers) *or* ½ yard each of 8 blue fabrics for piecing

BLUE *(Kona Nautical)*: ½ yard for binding

BACKING: 3 yards

Other materials

BATTING: 53″ × 68″

TEMPLATES: Make templates from these patterns: 3″ Convex (page 122) and 3″ Concave (page 125).

TIP

If you'd like to use a printed stripe fabric instead of piecing the stripes, see Printed Stripe Option (page 121).

CUTTING

See Cutting Techniques (page 13) for more information about how to cut curves and use fabric efficiently. See the cutting diagram for convex pieces (page 14).

FABRIC	CUT	SUBCUT	
		Rectangles, squares, and strips	3″ convex
Pink	1 rectangle 45″ × 31″	Mark 4″ from the upper right and 10″ from lower left corners. Cut in half diagonally from the marks.	
Yellow	5 strips 3½″ × WOF*		58
Blue strips	Trim 60 precut strips to 1½″ × WOF. If you bought 8 blue fabrics, cut 8 strips 1½″ × WOF from each fabric. You will need only 60 strips, but it's nice to have the design options.		

* WOF = width of fabric

CONSTRUCTION

See Piecing Basics (page 15) for more details about how to sew, press, and trim the curves and stripes for this quilt.

Follow directions in the sequence provided to keep colors organized.

Row A

1. Make a strip set with 6 blue strips in random order. Press the seams open.

2. Subcut a 6½″ × 6½″ square and 3 rectangles 6½″ × 10½″.

3. Align the 3″ concave template on the top left corner of the square and trim along the curve. Sew a yellow convex piece to the square.

4. Align the concave template with the top right corner of 1 rectangle and trim. Repeat to cut a curve at the top left corner. Sew a yellow convex piece into each curve.

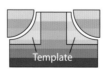

5. Repeat Step 4 to make a second rectangle with 2 yellow convex pieces.

Patio Lights, 45″ × 60″; designed, pieced, and quilted by Daisy Aschehoug; 2018

6. Align the concave template on the top right corner of the remaining rectangle and trim. Sew a yellow convex piece to the rectangle.

7. Sew the sections together to complete a Row A.

8. Repeat Steps 1–7 to make 4 total.

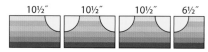

Row A

Row B

1. Sew a strip set with 6 blue strips in random order. Press the seams open.

2. Subcut 3 rectangles 6½″ × 10½″ and 1 rectangle 6½″ × 4½″.

3. Align the concave template on the top right corner of the 4½″ rectangle. Sew a yellow convex piece to the rectangle.

4. Align the concave template on the 2 top corners of a 10½″ rectangle and trim. Sew a yellow convex piece into each curve.

5. Repeat Step 4 to make a second rectangle with 2 yellow convex pieces.

6. Align the concave template on the top left corner of a 10½″ rectangle. Sew a yellow convex piece to the rectangle.

7. Sew the rectangles together to complete a Row B.

8. Repeat Steps 1–7 to make 4 total.

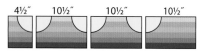

Row B

Rows C and F

1. Sew a strip set with 6 blue strips in random order. Press the seams open.

2. Subcut a 6½″ × 6½″ square and 3 rectangles 6½″ × 10½″ rectangles. Set aside 1 of the rectangles for Row F.

3. Align the concave template on the top left corner of the square and trim. Sew a yellow convex piece to the square.

4. Align the concave template on both top corners of a 10½″ rectangle and trim. Sew a yellow convex piece into each curve.

5. Align the concave template with the top right corner of the remaining 10½″ rectangle. Sew a yellow convex piece to the rectangle.

6. Sew the rectangles together to complete Row C.

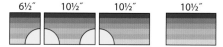

Rows C and F are created from one strip set.

Rows D and E

1. Sew a strip set with 6 blue strips in random order. Press the seams open.

2. Subcut 2 squares 6½″ × 6½″, 2 rectangles 6½″ × 10½″, and 1 rectangle 6½″ × 4½″.

3. Align the concave template on the top left corner of one square and trim. Sew a yellow convex piece to the square.

4. Align the concave template to the top right corner of a 10½″ rectangle and trim. Sew a yellow convex piece to the rectangle.

5. Sew the square and rectangle together to complete Row D.

6. Rotate the remaining rectangles and squares so that you are cutting the concave corners from the other side of the strip set. Align the concave template with the top right corner of a 4½″ rectangle and trim. Sew a yellow convex piece to the rectangle.

7. Align the concave template on both top corners of a 10½″ rectangle and trim. Sew a yellow convex piece into each curve.

8. Align the concave template with the top left corner of the remaining 6½″ × 6½″ square and trim. Sew a yellow convex piece to the rectangle.

9. Sew the rectangles together to complete Row E.

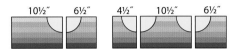

Rows D and E are created from one strip set. Using templates on opposite sides for each row will help rows look as though they were created from different strip sets.

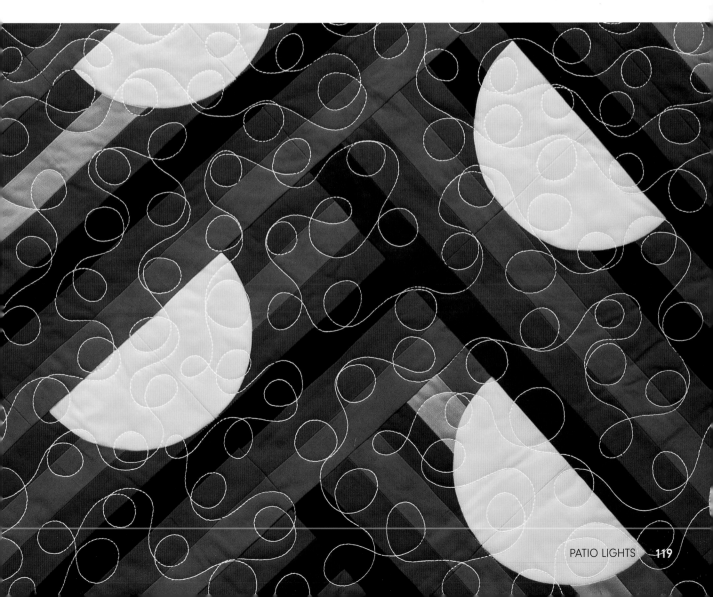

Quilt Construction

Refer to the quilt assembly and trimming diagram.

1. Arrange the rows and pink pieces as shown. Starting at the bottom of the quilt, sew Row D to Row F.

2. Sew Row E to the right side of DF.

3. Sew Row C to the left side of DEF.

4. Sew Row B to right side of CDEF.

5. Sew Row A to left side of BCDEF.

6. Continue the pattern to add the remaining A and B rows.

7. Sew pink diagonal Piece 1 to the top right of the rows, matching the diagonal edge to the row unit. Trim the left edge of the pink piece even with the left side of the rows unit.

8. Sew pink diagonal Piece 2 to the top left side of the rows.

9. Align your ruler ½″ from the edge of the yellow half-circles to square the quilt up to 45½″ × 60½″.

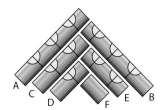

Finishing

Layer, quilt, and bind as desired.

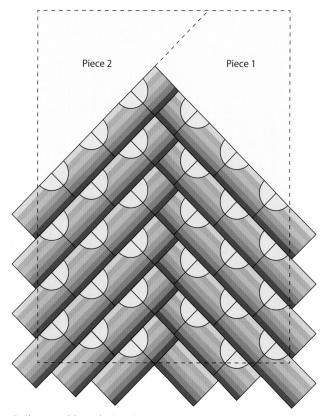

Quilt assembly and trimming

PRINTED STRIPE OPTION

To use a striped print, buy 2 yards for fabric with stripes perpendicular to the selvage or 2⅓ yards for fabric with stripes parallel to the selvage

Skip Step 1 on all Row Assembly instructions. Instead, cut 10 strips 6½″ × the width of fabric. Follow the instructions for pieced stripes but as you construct each row, skip Step 1 and go directly to Step 2 to subcut the striped units.

Patio Lights, 45″ × 60″; designed, pieced, and quilted by Daisy Aschehoug; 2018

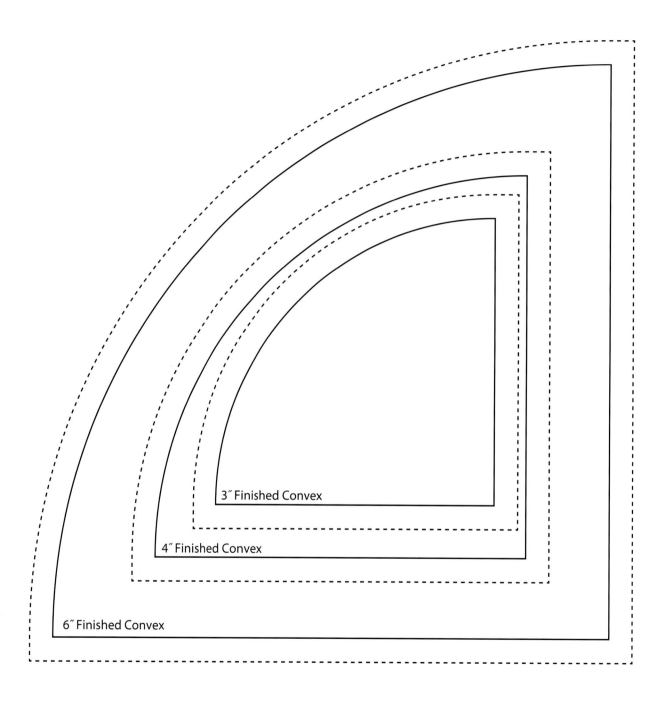

3″ Finished Convex

4″ Finished Convex

6″ Finished Convex

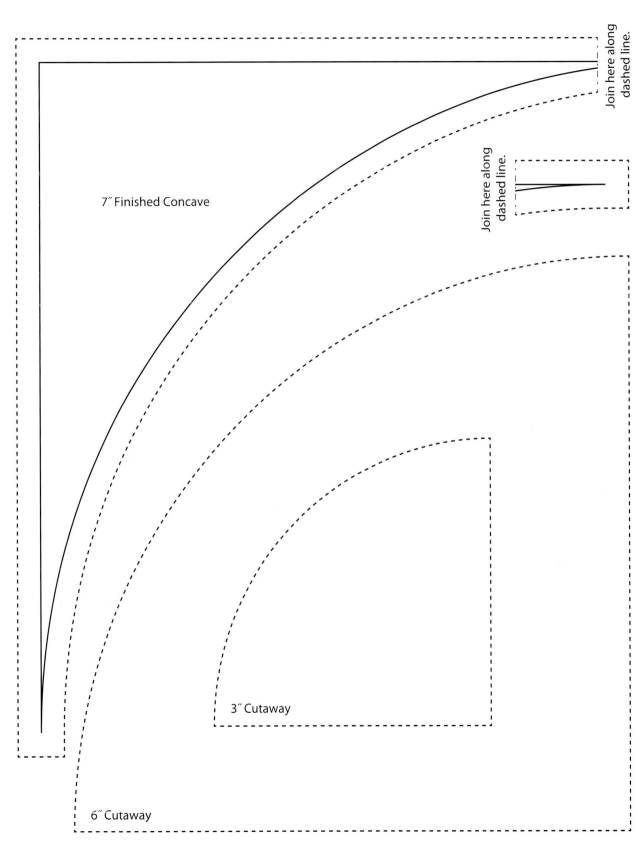

7″ Finished Concave

Join here along dashed line.

Join here along dashed line.

3″ Cutaway

6″ Cutaway

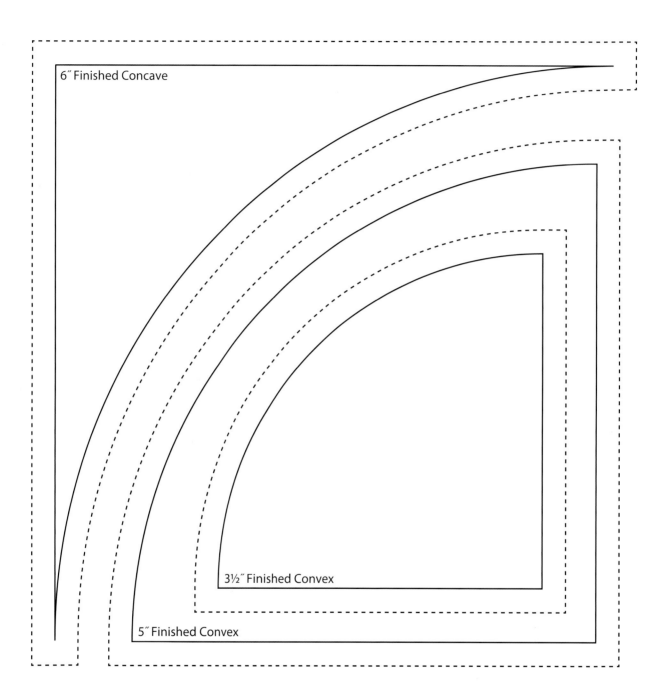

6″ Finished Concave

3½″ Finished Convex

5″ Finished Convex

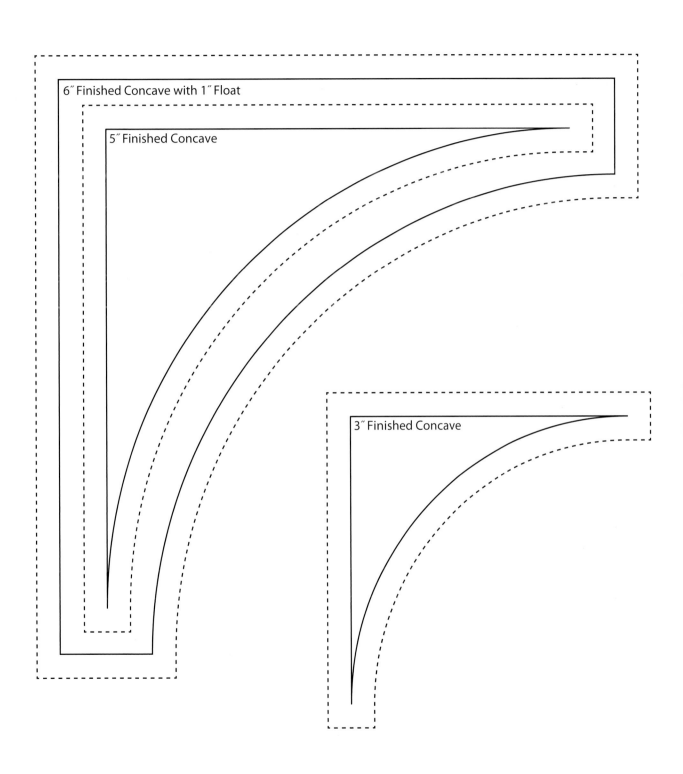

6″ Finished Concave with 1″ Float

5″ Finished Concave

3″ Finished Concave

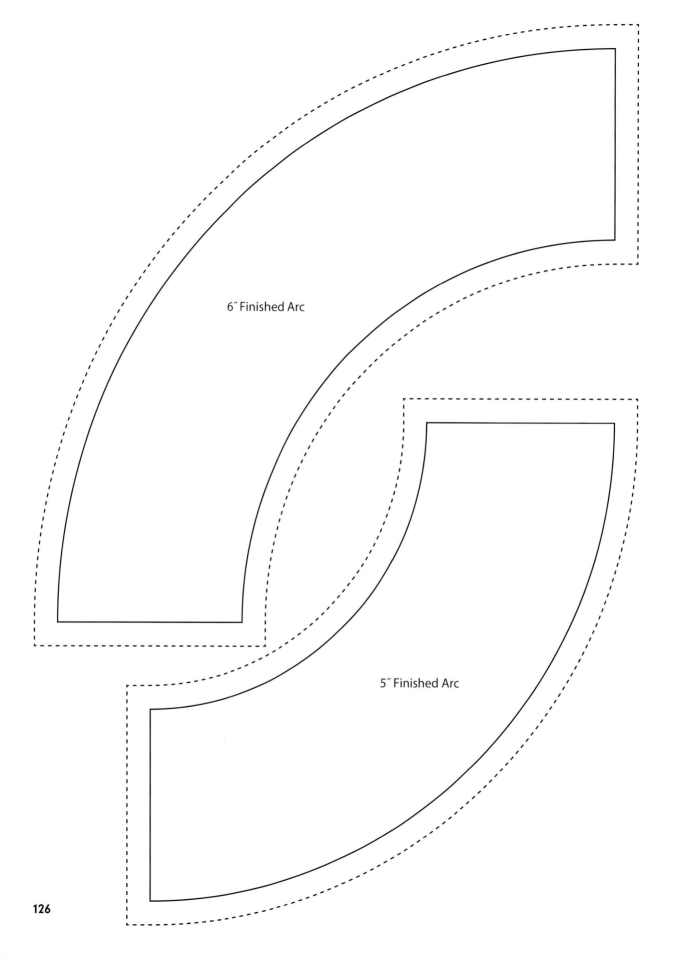

6″ Finished Arc

5″ Finished Arc

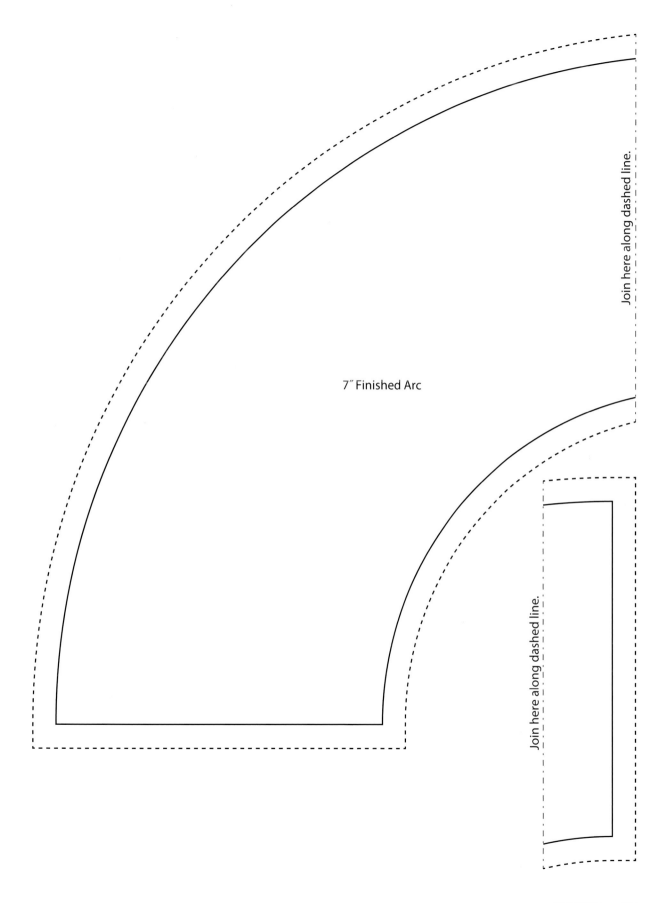

7″ Finished Arc

Join here along dashed line.

Join here along dashed line.

ABOUT THE AUTHORS

Photo by Jennifer Clouse

Photo by Barbora Kurcova

HEATHER BLACK first tried quilting in 1995 but didn't catch the quilting bug until 2011 when she designed, pieced, and hand quilted her first queen-size quilt. Shortly after that she discovered modern quilting and from that point on Heather has been designing and making quilts whenever possible.

Her quilts and patterns have been featured in various quilting publications, and Heather is an active member in various local guilds including the Modern Quilt Guild. She has had myriad quilts displayed at international, national, and regional quilt shows. Her quilts have hung at International Quilt Festivals Houston and Chicago, AQS Fall QuiltWeek, QuiltCon, MQX Midwest, and many more. She won first place use of negative space for her *Urban Trek* quilt at QuiltCon 2018 and several ribbons in regional and local shows.

Along with quilting, Heather is a single widowed mom of a beautiful young girl, CoraJoan, and lives in Spokane, Washington. She grew up in the Pacific Northwest and attended college in Pennsylvania.

DAISY ASCHEHOUG's quilts have been published in *Modern Quilts Unlimited*, *Love Patchwork and Quilting*, *Simply Moderne*, and *Modern Patchwork*. She's won awards and has projects included in multiple compilations. Before quilting, Daisy guided rafts, fought wildfires, and facilitated contentious natural resource management plans. As a recent expat living with her husband and two sons in Norway, she is currently planning how to travel through Europe while sharing her love of quilting.

Visit the authors online and follow on social media!

Heather:
Website: quiltachusetts.com
Instagram: @quiltachusetts

Daisy:
Website: warmfolk.com
Instagram: @warmfolk